TABLE OF CONTENTS

Top 20 Test Taking Tips

1. Carefully follow all the test registration procedures
2. Know the test directions, duration, topics, question types, how many questions
3. Setup a flexible study schedule at least 3-4 weeks before test day
4. Study during the time of day you are most alert, relaxed, and stress free
5. Maximize your learning style; visual learner use visual study aids, auditory learner use auditory study aids
6. Focus on your weakest knowledge base
7. Find a study partner to review with and help clarify questions
8. Practice, practice, practice
9. Get a good night's sleep; don't try to cram the night before the test
10. Eat a well balanced meal
11. Know the exact physical location of the testing site; drive the route to the site prior to test day
12. Bring a set of ear plugs; the testing center could be noisy
13. Wear comfortable, loose fitting, layered clothing to the testing center; prepare for it to be either cold or hot during the test
14. Bring at least 2 current forms of ID to the testing center
15. Arrive to the test early; be prepared to wait and be patient
16. Eliminate the obviously wrong answer choices, then guess the first remaining choice
17. Pace yourself; don't rush, but keep working and move on if you get stuck
18. Maintain a positive attitude even if the test is going poorly
19. Keep your first answer unless you are positive it is wrong
20. Check your work, don't make a careless mistake

Corrections Officer Exam

Corrections

The term "corrections" encompasses the act of incarcerating and rehabilitating offenders. It also refers to the agencies and programs that are responsible for these programs. Each state has a government agency that is responsible for the corrections function in that state. This agency operates the state's prisons and manages other corrections programs. The structure and management of these agencies varies from state-to-state.

An agency administrator, typically appointed by the governor, oversees the functions of the department. The department sets the policies that govern all of the institutions and programs under its jurisdiction. There are approximately 1,100 state confinement facilities in the United States and another 300 to 400 community corrections programs.

Criminal justice system

The criminal justice system consists of law enforcement, courts, and corrections institutions. Law enforcement is responsible for investigating crimes, gathering evidence, and making arrests. Prosecutors, who are part of law enforcement, represent the state in court, arguing for conviction and sentencing.

Courts are responsible for balancing enforcement of the law against the rights of the accused. Trial courts manage the trial of criminal matters, with a jury if requested by the accused. If the accused is found guilty, he may be sentenced to probation, a fine, or incarceration in a jail or prison. There are at least two levels of appellate court above every trial court, including the United States Supreme Court. Finally, corrections agencies are responsible for punishment and rehabilitation.

Standards

No single set of correctional standards applies throughout the United States. In 1870, the National Prison Congress met and developed the first set of principles and objectives for prison operations. This group later became the American Correctional Association (ACA), a private, non-profit organization.

The ACA has expanded those early principles and objectives into a comprehensive set of standards. Membership in the ACA is voluntary, as is compliance with the association's standards. About 10% of federal prisons and 44% of state prisons are accredited by the ACA. The Bureau of Prisons has adopted regulations and administrative procedures that provide standards for federal prisons. Some states have also adopted formal standards. The federal and states standards are based in great part on the ACA's standards.

Facility accreditation

Facility accreditation refers to a review of the prison for compliance with corrections standards. The review may be conducted by a federal, state, or local government agency or it may be conducted by a private organization, such as the ACA or its affiliate, the Commission on Accreditation for Corrections (CAC). Accreditation standards address services, programs, and operations. Factors considered typically include physical plant, safety and emergency procedures, sanitation, food service, staff training, inmate discipline, and financial operations.

In the federal prison system, or in states that have adopted accreditation standards, accreditation is mandatory. In other facilities, accreditation is voluntary and the facility itself must initiate the process by contacting the accrediting organization and requesting an audit.

National Commission on Correctional Health Care (NCCHC)

The NCCHC is a nonprofit organization created by the American Medical Association in 1970, in cooperation with a number of other organizations and associations interested in correctional health care. The NCCHC has developed voluntary, national standards for health services in prisons, jails, and juvenile facilities. The standards address care and treatment, health records, administration, personnel, and medical-legal issues.

The NCCHC offers accreditation of prison health care services, also on a voluntary basis. More recently, the NCCHC has started offering accreditation of opioid treatment programs. This accreditation allows facilities to obtain required certification from the federal Substance Abuse and Mental Health Services Administration (SAMHSA). The Commission also offers certification of prison healthcare professionals.

Audits

An audit is a review of facility or agency records or procedures. An audit may be conducted by an agency employee – an *internal* audit – or by an outside person or organization – an *external* audit. Audit goals vary widely. Financial audits are mathematical double-checks. The auditor cross-checks financial records to ensure their accuracy. Records audits also involve cross-checking, but they involve information, not finances. Finally, procedures audits check that (a) the appropriate procedures have been adopted; and (b) the adopted procedures are followed. Upon completion of the audit, the auditor prepares a report and submits it to the requesting entity. Prison audits may be requested by prison administration, a prison board of trustees, a higher-level office (such as the governor), or by the state legislature.

Male inmate population

There are about 2 million males incarcerated in the United States, the highest incarceration rate in the developed world.
- Race: About 35% of the male prison population is white, 20% is Hispanic, 36% is African-American, and 4% is Asian or other.
- Age: The majority of male inmates are between the ages of 20 and 30.
- Offense: About half of male inmates are serving time for a violent offense, 20% for a property crime (such as theft), and 20% for drugs.

In addition, about 5% of the inmates in state prison are not US citizens. The number increases to 20% in federal prisons. About 12% are serving in federal prisons, with about 60% in state prisons, and the remainder (28%) in local jails.

Female inmate population

There are about 180,000 females serving time in state and federal prisons and local jails – almost 8% of the total prison population. The incarceration rate for women is increasing faster than the incarceration rate for men.

The female prison population can be summed up by a rule of two-thirds:
- Race: roughly two thirds are minority (African-American or Hispanic)
- Age: roughly two-thirds of female inmates are less than 35 years old
- Offense: roughly two-thirds are serving time for property (e.g., theft) and drug offenses.

In addition, roughly two-thirds of female inmates are parents of minor children. About 5% of female prisoners are pregnant at the time of incarceration.

Juvenile justice corrections program

There are about 100,000 offenders in juvenile facilities. All juveniles are in state prisons, because federal prisons do not accept minors. The age at which a minor can be incarcerated with adult inmates is 18 in most states, but some states process offenders who are 17 years old as adults and a handful process offenders as young as 16 years old as adults. Once a minor is committed to a juvenile facility, he or she may remain in the system until the age of 21.

Juvenile facilities are subject to the federal Juvenile Justice and Delinquency Prevention Act, which was passed in 1974 and reauthorized in 2002. The JJDPA establishes four "protections" for minor offenders: (1) reducing commitment for status crimes (e.g., runaways); (2) separating minors from adult offenders; (3) removing minors from adult jails; and (4) reducing the disproportionate number of minorities in the system.

Problems in prison population

Inmates are more likely to be educationally-disadvantaged. About 10% have a learning or speech disability and less than one-third had completed high school at the time of incarceration

Inmates are more likely to have mental health problems. About one-half have symptoms of mental illness or mood disorder. Approximately one in eight receives mental health services, with about ten percent receiving medicine for such conditions as depression, anxiety, and schizophrenia. In addition, about two-thirds have a history of substance abuse.

Inmates are much more likely to have communicable diseases. It is estimated that as much as 20% of the inmate population is positive for hepatitis B virus

(HBV). Inmates are about 4 times as likely to test positive for tuberculosis (TB). About 3% of female and 2% of male inmates are positive for the human immunodeficiency virus (HIV). Many inmates arrive at prison infected by other sexually-transmitted diseases (STDs).

Federal prison system

The federal prison system is run by the Bureau of Prisons (BOP), an agency of the Department of Justice. The BOP is responsible for incarceration of inmates who have been convicted of federal laws and of felony violations of the Code of the District of Columbia. The BOP also administers military prisons. The BOP also contracts with private corrections companies, state prisons, and jails to handle inmates in special situations or where the federal prisons lack capacity.

The BOP includes the National Institute of Corrections (NIC). The NIC provides training, technical assistance, information services, and program development assistance to federal, state, and local institutions. NIC maintains a library of resources and information regarding corrections.

Private corrections industry

Private companies may take over the operations of government prisons, or they may build private prisons and contract with government agencies to house offenders in those prisons. Fees are calculated on a per-person, per-day basis. Private prison management was popular during the 1980s. Proponents of private prisons argue that they are more efficient and not hampered by laws and regulations applicable to government employers. Opponents argue that private prisons cut corners, are more susceptible to corruption, and are not as stable because the company operating the prison might go out of business. They also assert that the fee structure discourages early release programs. The largest private corrections firms in the United States are the Corrections Corporation of America (CCA), the GEO Group, and the Cornell Companies.

The Auburn System

The Auburn System was an approach to corrections developed at the Auburn Penitentiary in New York in the early 1800s. Its predecessor, the Pennsylvania System, involved solitary confinement of inmates so that they could reflect on their crimes. The Auburn System, by contrast, provided for communal work and eating areas, with single-occupancy cells used only for sleeping. The Auburn System carried forward the Pennsylvania System's requirement of strict silence. Moreover, harsh discipline was used to maintain order in common areas. Inmates who did not follow the rules were sent into permanent solitary confinement, which often led to mental breakdowns. The concept of cells as sleeping areas and a central common area where prisoners could congregate has been carried forward into modern times.

Boot camp

A boot camp – or regimented treatment program -- is an alternative to traditional incarceration for young, first-time offenders. Boot camps use military training techniques to "shock" or rehabilitate offenders and introduce them to structure and discipline. Boot camps are most widely used for juvenile offenders and often only the consent of the parent – and not of the inmate – is required. A short-term sentence in a boot camp can substitute for a longer sentence in a traditional prison. The overall concept is behavior modification, but boot camps may also include educational and substance abuse programs. Boot camps were outlawed in Florida in 2006 after corrections officers inadvertently suffocated an offender by putting ammonia tablets in his nostrils in an attempt to revive him after he collapsed.

Direct supervision

With modern "indirect" supervision, corrections officers are separated from inmates by physical barriers, such as a secure control booth. One or more officers monitor a "pod" of inmates and operate control systems. This technique increases officer safety, but its efficacy as an inmate management technique has been questioned. With direct supervision, a corrections officer works in a pod with the inmates to manage their behavior. The officer moves throughout the unit and usually uses a desk in the common area, rather than a secure control booth. Therefore, the officer has direct contact with each inmate. The officer is responsible for recognizing and defusing problems before they get out of hand.

Unit management approach

Unit management is a team approach to corrections, started by the Bureau of Prisons. It is now used it virtually every federal prison. The prison is divided into groups of 200 to 300 inmates. Management and decision-making performed on a unit basis, with each unit operating as a mini-prison within the larger facility. Multidisciplinary teams consisting of unit managers, caseworkers, officers, and other professionals are assigned to each unit and office in the unit. Each inmate remains in the unit for most of his sentence. The increased and long-term contact between inmates and staff fosters interpersonal relationships. Moreover, staff is able to make more knowledgeable decisions about treatment and specialized programs for each inmate.

Communicating policies to inmates

Upon arrival, each inmate should be provided with a copy of the unit's rules and regulations and the institution's policies should be reviewed with the inmate. In addition, each housing unit should have a method of communicating the following information:

- Inmate rights and responsibilities;
- Inmate grievance policy;
- Housekeeping policy and procedures;
- Hygiene and personal appearance policy;
- Personal property matrix;
- Inmate mail policy;
- Disciplinary rules and sanctions for violations;
- Fire evacuation plan;
- Visitation rules and schedule;
- Program and activity schedule;
- Schedule for religious services;
- Escorted leave schedule;
- Other relevant information.

This information may be posted on a bulletin board in the common area.

Emergency plans

An emergency plan should address the following:

- Definition: The plan should specify what constitutes an "emergency" and who has authority to declare an emergency. The list will usually include any situation where there is threat to human life, large-scale destruction of property, or a risk of loss of control of the institution. The list may also include major labor problems, such as a strike, and natural disasters.
- Response: The plan should set forth steps for responding to the emergency, including establishing a command post, chain of command, and assistance from outside agencies.

- Notifications: The plan should specify who is to be notified outside of the prison when there is an emergency. This includes notices to the media, where appropriate.
- Training: The plan should set forth the annual training requirements, including the types of training and how often training will occur.

Civil disturbances

A civil disturbance is unrest outside of the institution, involving civilians, such as a protest or riot. The disturbance may be directed at the institution, such as death penalty protests, or it may be unrelated, such as the riots in Los Angeles after the Rodney King verdict.

Civil disturbances pose three types of risk to the institution. First, the disturbance might block access to the institution, creating problems with staffing and supplies. Second, civilians might target the institution for violence, or the disturbance may disrupt vital resources, such as electricity. Third, the disturbance may spread to the inmates, or may cause stress or concern among the inmates. The institution should have a civil disturbance plan that addresses each of these risks. The plan should address communications with outside law enforcement and the authority of corrections officers to arrest civilians who enter the institution.

Work or food strikes

Work or food strikes signal serious discontent among inmates. In a large-scale strike, the fact that inmates are acting in concert increases the risk that the strike will progress to a mass disturbance. Accordingly, the institution should respond quickly to identify the reason for the protest and address inmate concerns to the extent possible. First, officers should be alert to signs of an impending strike. Hunger strikes are often announced in advance. Second, officers should determine the cause of the strike and should identify the strike's leaders. Third, inmates should be encouraged to use the institution's grievance procedure to address their complaints. Fourth, health care personnel should be alerted to the risk of a hunger strike as early as possible so that they can monitor the mental and physical status of the inmates.

Mass staff sick call or staff strikes

Administration will have to address staff complaints while maintaining institution security. First, administration should determine the source of staff discontent as soon as possible and take appropriate action to address the complaints. Staff should be encouraged to use formal grievance procedures. Second, administration should address institution security. Staffing should be analyzed to determine which posts can be temporarily shut down and which programs can be suspended without adverse effect on inmate morale and security. Third, administration should address other sources of personnel. Staff members who continue to report to work may be called on to work extra hours. Administration may also be able to obtain assistance from other institutions or law enforcement. Fifth, administration should communicate with inmates about the status of the strike and should be alert to inmates who will try to take advantage of the situation.

Natural or civil disasters

A natural disaster (tornado, hurricane, earthquake, etc.) or civil disaster (bombing or declaration of war) may threaten the physical plant of the institution and cause stress to inmates. It can also disrupt staffing and supplies. The institution should have in place a plan that addresses:

- Information: Administration, or a designee, should remain in contact with outside authorities throughout the situation to make sure that the institution has current information.

- Internal Communication: Administration should regularly communicate status to staff and inmates and provide updates as appropriate.
- Records Protection: The plan should address preservation of records that could affect the rights of any person.
- Evacuation: The plan should set forth procedures for evacuation.
- Staffing and supplies: The plan should address procedures for dealing with staffing shortages, along the lines of the institution's plan for dealing with a staff strike, supply shortages, and disruption of utilities.

Housekeeping plans

The housekeeping plan should address common areas, cells, and inmate hygiene:
- Common areas: Inmates should be assigned cleaning duties in the common areas.
- Cells: Cells should be cleaned daily, including making the bed, and picking litter and debris up off the floor. Inmates should be in compliance with the institution's policy regarding personal property.
- Inmate hygiene: All inmates should have access to toilet facilities and hot and cold running water 24 hours a day. The plan should address showering. The institution should provide hair care services.
- Inmate laundry: The plan should address access to laundry facilities within the institution or nearby.
- Inspections: The plan should provide for inspection of common areas and cells at least once each week.
- Discipline: The plan, or another policy, should set forth the discipline for violations of housekeeping and hygiene standards.

Bomb plans

A bomb plan should address the following:

- Threat reporting: Most bomb threats are received by telephone, but threats may also be sent in writing through the mail or e-mail. Staff should document the nature of the threat, the means by which it was communicated, the time and date of receipt, and any other useful information.

- Communication: Staff should alert law enforcement and should also inform all staff members if a bomb is located or if a bomb threat is received.

- Detection: The plan should address the response if an officer locates a bomb or suspected bomb. Officers should never attempt to move a bomb. The plan should address reducing sources of electrical energy or radio signals in the prison that might activate the bomb.

- Evacuation: The plan should address evacuation of inmates and staff.

- Training: The plan should specify any required training regarding bombs and bomb threats.

Mass disturbance plans

A *mass disturbance* or *riot* is one of the most serious crises for a corrections institution due the risk of personal injury, property destruction, and loss of control. The plan should address:

- Communication: The incident should immediately be communicated within the unit, institution, and department. The plan should also address communication to outside authorities and, where appropriate, the media.

- Command: The chain of command should be clearly set forth. Commanders should provide for isolation of the disturbance as soon as possible.

- Staffing: Circumstances under which additional staff should be called in to assist should be specified.
- Assault team: An assault team should be assembled to retake control. The plan should address tactical methods.
- Regular operations: The plan should identify who will be responsible for maintaining normal operations in the rest of the facility so that other inmates do not suffer due to the actions of those participating in the disturbance.

Procedures for restoring normalcy after a mass disturbance should address inmate needs, physical plant, staff needs, investigation and discipline, and a report.
- Inmates: There should be a full count of inmates in the institution. Medical personnel should be available to address medical and psychological issues.
- Physical plant: Areas that were damaged, where gas was used, or that are otherwise not habitable should be evacuated. Arrangements should be made for facility repairs and replacement of any destroyed property.
- Staff needs: There should be a full count of staff. Medical personnel should be available to address medical and psychological issues.
- Investigation and discipline: There should be a full investigation and evidence should be collected. Discipline proceedings should be conducted for all those involved.
- Report: A full report should be prepared. The report should address any recommended changes to procedures.

Escape plans

An escape plan should address:
- Confirmation and containment: Officers should confirm that one or more inmates are missing. A full inmate count should be conducted and the facility should be thoroughly searched. A suspected escape should

- 18 -

be reported throughout the institution immediately, especially to perimeter guards.

- Escapee identification packet: Once the escape is confirmed, an identification packet should be assembled on each missing inmate.
- Notification: A suspected escape should immediately be reported to administration. The plan should specify which outside agencies should be notified of the escape, including state and local law enforcement and, where appropriate, the media. Victim notification procedures should be followed. "Wanted" flyers should be posted and distributed.
- Escapee recovery: The plan should specify procedures for assembling recovery teams, use of fugitive apprehension agents, and jurisdictional issues.
- Escape warrant: The district attorney should be contacted about filing escape charges.

Hostage plans

A hostage plan should address the following:
- Communication: Officers should report hostage situations immediately to a supervisor. The officer who first learns of the situation should not attempt to negotiate with the hostage taker. The plan should specify procedures for notifying the hostage's family members.
- Negotiation team: The plan should identify a negotiation team. Members of the team should receive specialized training.
- Loss of authority: The plan should specify that any employee taken hostage immediately loses any administrative authority to issue directives to others.
- Non-negotiable matters: The plan should set forth any items that are not negotiable, such as release.
- Hostage training: All staff members should be trained on appropriate hostage behavior.

- Institution security: The plan should specify any special security measures that will be observed, such as securing the area and putting the remainder of the institution under lock-down or other special status.

ACA standards for fire prevention

The ACA standards for fire protection address the following:

- Inspections: The standards require regular equipment inspections by internal personnel and inspection by external authorities at least once each year.
- Training: Staff should be trained in the use of fire extinguishers and basic fire suppression techniques. The institution should pursue joint training exercises with local firefighting agencies. Joint exercises at the institution allow outside firefighters to become familiar with the facility's layout.
- Equipment: The standard calls for safety equipment pursuant to the Life Safety Code of the National Fire Protection Association, including extinguishers, hoses, nozzles, water supplies, and sprinklers. The institution should have access to a fire truck.
- Alarms: The institution should have adequate emergency alarms, smoke detectors, and equipment to notify hearing- and vision-impaired inmates.
- Evacuation plan: Each facility should have a written evacuation plan. A certified inspector should review the plan.

Fire plans

A fire plan should address the following:

- Notification: The plan should list persons to be contacted -- internal and external – in the event of a fire

- Personnel: Each facility should have at least one designated staff member who is responsible for compliance with the fire plan. In addition, the plan should set forth eligibility criteria for inmates to serve as fire crew.
- Equipment: Each institution should have adequate safety equipment, including extinguishers and hoses.
- Inspections: Safety equipment should be inspected regularly.
- Evacuation: Each facility should have a diagram of fire evacuation routes.
- Security: The plan should set forth security procedures during an evacuation.
- Training: All employees should receive training on the fire plan and the evacuation routes.
- Drills: Fire drills should be conducted at least one time each month. Inmates should participate to the extent feasible.

Preventing fires is easier than suppressing them. Prevention strategies include:
- Smoking: Non-combustible receptacles should be provided in outside smoking areas, as well as inside, if smoking is permitted indoors.
- Flammable liquids: Inmates should use flammable liquids only under supervision and in the minimum quantities possible. Storage cabinets should be fireproof. Rags used with flammable liquids should be disposed of in non-combustible containers.
- Electrical hazards: Inmates and employees should be alert to altered or overloaded electrical outlets. Unauthorized appliances and extension cords also pose a hazard.
- Trash: Proper storage and disposal of trash is necessary to reduce the amount of combustible material.
- Mattresses: Especially where inmates are allowed to smoke indoors, mattresses should be of a material that meets the flammability standards set forth in the Life Safety Code.

Utility failure plans

A utility failure plan should include the following:

- Definition: The plan should distinguish between minimal or isolated utility failures and severe utility failures – those that impact safety, health, or welfare of staff or inmates.
- Notification: The plan should provide for notification of administration if there is a severe utility failure, including the identification of the administrator responsible for determining whether additional staff or equipment is necessary. The plan should provide for notifying the utility provider.
- Vital operations: The plan should identify those utility-dependent functions at each facility – such as electrical fences -- that cannot be interrupted. Provisions should be made to maintain continuity of these functions during a utility failure. Electricity generating equipment should be available for vital functions.
- Utility diagrams: Diagrams of utility systems should be accessible to facility location of the problem and repairs.

Prison chaplains

Prison chaplains are the spiritual counselors of the correctional system. Chaplains are typically staff officers, paid by the county or state that runs the prison. In some states, the chaplain function is outsourced. There may be one, two, or more chaplains assigned to a prison, and these employees may work either full- or part-time.

The qualifications for prison chaplains vary, but most institutions require at least a four-year college degree and religious training, either formal or informal. Some institutions also require chaplains to have experience with counseling.

Prison chaplains must usually have "denominational endorsement," which is support from a specific, organized religion. However, all chaplains are expected to be "interdenominational." This means they must provide religious support for all of the religions practiced by inmates.

The general duties of prison chaplains fall into the following categories: religious services, religious education, counseling, coordination of internal staff, coordination of external resources, and public relations.

Prison chaplains conduct interdenominational religious services for all inmates. They are also responsible for religious education. In this respect, chaplains maintain libraries of religious books and other resources for inmates of all religions.

Prison chaplains counsel inmates, their families, and even staff members. If there is a death in an inmate's family, the prison chaplain is responsible for breaking the news to the inmate and providing grief counseling. Prison chaplains also counsel inmates who are suicidal. They receive letters from inmate families and they counsel family members who come to visit inmates. Prison chaplains coordinate resources, both internal and external. Internally, a prison chaplain may have a staff. The chaplain will also work closely with the corrections officers in the institution, relying on them for information about inmates who need special assistance. Externally, the prison chaplain will respond to inquiries from outside ministers and arrange for their visits to the prison.

Prison chaplains must balance their duties as spiritual advisors with their correctional responsibilities. As staff officers, prison chaplains may be called on to advise management about security matters. This may include arranging security passes for inmates who wish to attend services or security so an inmate can attend the funeral of a close relative.

As spiritual advisors, prison chaplains must be neutral about the religious choices of the inmates, while providing guidance and support. This means chaplains must support, and not disparage, each inmate's religion. Prison chaplains provide or arrange for religious ceremonies, such as baptism, communion, and last rites.

To establish relationships with inmates, chaplains circulate throughout the prison on a regular basis, including the yard, visiting areas, and the infirmary. They also maintain offices where inmates can counsel in private.

Like the chaplain, the corrections officer must maintain a balance between the religious rights of inmates and the officer's correctional responsibilities. Corrections staff must never disparage any matter relating to inmate religious practices, including an inmate's religion, religious practices, religious services at the prison, and the prison chaplain. Moreover, corrections officers should recognize that the chaplain is an important source of support for inmates. Officers should encourage inmates who are going through unusually tough times or difficulties to visit the prison chaplain. In some cases, it may be appropriate to ask the chaplain to check on a particular inmate.

On the other hand, officers are responsible for providing security, even during religious services. Most institutions require an officer to be present during services. An officer assigned to chapel duty should maintain neutrality and not interfere with the services unless there is a security problem.

Finally, officers should respect the confidences between chaplains and the inmates. Chaplains' conversations with inmates are confidential. Chaplains do not have a duty to disclose their conversations with inmates unless necessary to prevent serious injury to the inmates or others. Accordingly, officer should not ask or expect chaplains to disclose their conversations with inmates.

Corrections office job positions

A corrections officer is responsible for maintaining security and order in an assigned area. This may include cellblocks, the yard, classrooms, the chapel, and work areas. New officers may be assigned to posts with limited inmate contact. They work under close supervision and have little or no authority to make independent judgments.

As officers gain experience and confidence, they progress to more inmate contact and direct inmate custody. More senior officers rotate through supervision of work detail, living quarters, recreational activities, and other inmate activities. Assignments requiring advanced skills include intake, work release, dealing with inmates with serious behavior problems, structured treatment, and rehabilitation programs. Some senior officers may also have responsibility for training new officers.

Corrections officer rights and duties

Officers of the law have the same rights and privileges afforded to every citizen by the Constitution. Officers are free to join labor unions, and may enjoy federal protections in this capacity. There are also a number of other laws specifically designed to protect the rights of state and federal employees. These include the Family Medical Leave Act, which gives employees the right to take medical leave, and the Fair Labor Standards Act, which describes when employees are owed overtime pay.

The standard duties of all officers are:

- Work Ethic: Officers must demonstrate strong work ethics. An officer should always be alert and attentive to duty: he should avoid distractions and notify a supervisor if he becomes sleepy or otherwise impaired while on duty.

- Relationships with Inmates: Officers must keep relationships with inmates on a professional level. Personal relationships undermine authority and security. For example, officers should not use nicknames when addressing inmates, give inmates gifts, accept anything from an inmate, or grant special privileges. If an officer recognizes an inmate or otherwise realizes that the officer knew the inmate before the inmate was incarcerated, the officer should report this to a supervisor.

- Monitoring of Inmates: Officers must be alert to changes in the prison community. An officer should note unusual activities or changes in daily routine, conduct, or appearance of one or more inmates. The officer should document these changes and report them to a supervisor.

Corrections officer responsibilities

The standard responsibilities of all officers are:

Respect for Authority: Officers must maintain respect for authority. The conduct of officers sets an example for inmates. Officers should address one another, and superiors, professionally and should respect the chain of command.

Reliability: Officers must be reliable. They must report to work on time and respond immediately when called in for overtime or during an emergency. If an officer is impaired in any manner, he should immediately tell a supervisor. Once at work, officers must remain at their posts until the next shift reports for duty.

<u>Personal Security</u>: In addition to their responsibility for prison security, officers must maintain personal security. By wearing regulation uniforms, employees identify themselves as officers. Moreover, officers are responsible for their personal items. An officer should secure his personal vehicle in the parking lot and should not bring any personal items to work unless absolutely necessary. When the officer arrives at his post, he should inspect the equipment and report any problems to a supervisor.

Corrections officers' rights

The rights of corrections officers depend on where they work. All officers are protected by the United States Constitution and federal laws, such as the Fair Labor Standards Act (minimum wage and overtime pay), that apply to all employees. Depending on the number of employees at the institution, officers may also be protected by Title VII, the Age Discrimination in Employment Act, and the Americans with Disabilities Act (anti-discrimination laws), and the Family Medical Leave Act.

In federal facilities and non-"right to work" states (such as Texas), officers may also be members of a union and have rights under a collective bargaining agreement (union contract). Moreover, even right-to-work states have laws protecting whistleblowers and workers' compensation claimants, among other things. An officer should become familiar with the labor laws in his or her state.

Code of Ethics

The Code of Ethics is a set of guiding principles, promulgated by the ACA, for corrections officers. It does not have the force of law unless it has been adopted into law by a particular state or other jurisdiction. However, it provides a frame of reference for corrections officers in carrying out their professional duties. Moreover, it extends to institutions and corrections officers who are members of the ACA.

In addition, many states and penal institutions have their own codes of ethics. States often require public employees to adhere to rules regarding conflicts of interest – relating to financial relationships -- and nepotism – relating to employment of relatives. These rules have the force of law and often carry criminal, as well as civil, penalties. An officer should be familiar with the applicable ethical rules in his state.

Part one: The Code declares that all corrections officers should make an effort to respect the civil and legal rights of other people at all times. Members of the ACA should never seek personal gain, but should make the benefit of other people the motivation for their professional activities. They should maintain solid working relationships with their colleagues in order to improve professional practice. They should avoid criticizing their colleagues publicly unless the criticism is warranted, constructive, and verifiable. They should respect the various disciplines at work in the criminal justice system, and should promote understanding between them. They should share information with the public as much as possible, so long as it does not infringe on the privacy of anyone

Part two: Members of the ACA are encouraged by the Code of Ethics to protect the rights of the members of the general public to be shielded from criminal activity. They should never use their professional position to obtain personal privileges, and should not allow personal interest to interfere with the performance of their duties. They should never enter into any situation that presents a possible conflict of interest, and should not accept any gifts or services that are improper or imply an obligation inconsistent with the effective and objective performance of duty. They should immediately report any corrupt or unethical behavior to the appropriate authorities.

Part three: Members of the American Corrections Association should always draw distinction between their personal views and the positions they take on behalf of an institution or the ACA. Members should never discriminate against any person because of that person's race, gender, creed, nationality, age, disability, or religious affiliation. They should preserve the integrity of private information and refrain from seeking any more information than is absolutely necessary to perform their duties. Members should make any necessary appointments, promotions, or dismissals according to the prevailing civil service rules, and on the basis of merit rather than personal interest. Finally, members of the ACA should always promote a workplace that is safe and healthy for all employees.

Ethical principals

The guiding principle for corrections officers is professionalism. Officers must balance their professional duties with their obligations toward inmates and their responsibilities to the public. In doing so, corrections officers are guided by the following ethical principles:

- promote respect for the profession
- respect other members of the criminal justice system
- report corrupt or unethical behavior
- refrain from using the officer's position for personal gain
- refrain from activities that are improper or have the appearance of impropriety
- refrain from accepting gifts or favors that may compromise the officer's professional duties
- do not engage in discrimination
- respect individual rights
- respect the public's right to information
- protect the public from criminal activity

Unethical behaviors

Unethical behaviors could include any of the following:

- Engaging in personal transactions with inmates or inmate relatives: selling, trading, bartering, giving, or receiving goods or services of any kind. This activity can compromise an officer's objectivity.

- Personal involvement with an inmate: familiarity with inmates can compromise an officer's objectivity. Officers should remain professional at all time and should not discuss their personal issues with inmates.

- Being under the influence of drugs or alcohol: intoxicants of any kind can delay reaction and impair an officer's effectiveness and judgment.

- Bringing contraband into the institution: Officers should not introduce contraband into the prison environment, including personal firearms, sharps, and personal electronic devices. This conduct creates unnecessary risk and contributes to the difficulty of controlling contraband within the institution.

- Fiscal improprieties, including the theft and misuse of inmate or institutional funds

- Abuse of inmates, whether physical, emotional, or sexual

- Inappropriate relationships with inmates, including bribery, conflict of interest, solicitation of gifts or favors

- On-duty misconduct, including insubordination, inattention to duty, breach of security, loss of temper, and gambling

- Off-duty misconduct, including any behavior that would adversely affect the officer's ability to perform his or her professional duties

- Investigative violations, including any attempts to cover up misconduct

Recognizing unethical behavior

Unethical behavior is often hard to detect, but an officer should be alert to indicators:

- Fraternization: on officer who is unduly familiar with inmates or employees of other law enforcement agencies
- Complaints: a pattern of complaints about an officer, an area of the institution, or supplies
- Lack of interest: an officer who seems uninterested in his work and is not responsive to legitimate needs of inmates
- Personal problems: an officer who has legal (civil, criminal), financial, physical, or mental problems

The proper reaction to unethical conduct should depend on the frequency and severity. Possible responses include:
- Expressing verbal disapproval
- Discussing continued problems with a supervisor
- Reporting violations to a supervisor
- Preventing criminal violations.

Whenever a credible complaint is made about an officer, the supervisor should investigate it fully. If it is determined that the complaint constitutes a criminal offense, the investigation should be turned over to another law enforcement agency. Once the evidence has been accumulated, it should only be given out as is necessary, and all witnesses should be required to sign an affidavit. If it will provide evidence, the subject in question may be put under surveillance. This surveillance may include peer monitoring, audiotape, or videotape. Near the end of the investigation, the subject should be interviewed. At all times, the rights of inmates and officers should be respected and protected.

"Code of silence"

The "code of silence" refers to an unwritten rule among officers to not report violations and to retaliate against those who do. It is widely recognized as one of the most serious problems facing the profession. The following methods are suggestions for breaking the "code of silence":

- Clarify that each employee's responsibilities include enforcements of rules, regulations, and ethical principals
- Adopt a clear mission statement and connect each employee's job to it
- Require accountability at all levels, enforced through regular audits
- Adopt a code of conduct and discipline sanctions for those who violate it
- Provide a means to report violations, anonymously if necessary

In addition, the highest levels of management must set an example through conduct that is without reproach.

Supervisor duties

Supervisors must be able to manage and communicate with their staff. Staff management includes planning staffing levels, scheduling post assignments, monitoring compliance with policies and procedures, managing supplies of equipment, providing feedback, formal and informal, administering staff discipline, and conducting written performance evaluations. Supervisors are also responsible for scheduling training for staff and participating in training themselves. In some cases, a supervisor may lead a training session.

Staff communication includes: making sure that the staff knows policies and procedures, communicating updates or changes to those policies and procedures, facilitating communication between shifts, and communicating to all staff about problems with inmates. Supervisors must also listen to complaints about staff and conduct or arrange for investigations.

As with their staffs, supervisors manage and communicate with inmates. They are responsible for ensuring enforcement of institution policies and rules with respect to inmates. They must maintain a presence in the facility and establish a rapport with inmates, so that inmates will approach them with questions or concerns. They may also authorize and schedule inmate programs.

Supervisors monitor inmate counts, manage inmate movement, and assist with restraint situations. They conduct security, safety, and health inspections. Supervisors also participate in determining classifications and may be required to testify at disciplinary and release proceedings. They are responsible for written reports and documentation of incidents.

Supervisors manage crises. The mediate disputes between inmates and staff or between inmates, and they initiate emergency procedures.

Chain of command

The term "chain of command," which originated in the military, refers to the hierarchical structure of authority and responsibility. Generally, one person in the chain of command take orders only from the person immediately above him and gives orders only to those below him. Corrections officers in prisons follow the chain of command system.

In a chain of command system, the manager in charge of the line personnel is called a "front line supervisor." If a line employee has a complaint, he is required to address the complaint first to a front line supervisor. If the front line supervisor is unresponsive, the employee is permitted to go to the next person in the chain of command.

Firearms

A corrections officer may use a rifle, a shotgun, or a handgun. A rifle is a long-barreled, single-shot firearm. A shotgun is a long-barreled, multiple-shot firearm.

Under most circumstances, two hands are required for operation of a long-barreled firearm. A handgun is a pistol or similar firearm that can be held and operated with one hand.

Each of these firearms has advantages and disadvantages. Handguns are small and so easier to carry. However, they are not very accurate. Rifles are more accurate, but they fire only one bullet. Shotguns spray pellets, and so cover a large area. For this reason, a shotgun may hit more than the intended target.

In the corrections context, the goal is to slow down or scare the target, not to cause serious injury. For this reason, the best strategy is often to shoot near the target or at the ground by the target.

Pat-down search procedures

Procedures for pat-down searches vary from institution to institution. Thus, the most important thing is to make sure you know the procedures that apply to your job.

There are some things that most pat-downs searches have in common. The inmate should be instructed to remove any loose items from his pockets or clothing for inspection. The inmate should also remove any outer layers of clothing, such as hats, sweaters, and coats.

After these steps, the officer uses his open hand to pat down the outer layer of the inmate's clothing and the inmate's person to determine whether the inmate has any contraband. The officer should be alert the possibility that the inmate is concealing needles or other sharp objects in his clothing. In the corrections setting, the officer may also wear latex gloves during the search.

Inmate intake procedures

Intake procedures address identification, orientation, assessment of needs and risks, and case management. The officer should confirm the identity of the inmate, and take photographs and fingerprints. The officer should provide the inmate with the institution's rules and procedures, as well as the prison address for correspondence. The inmate should be searched for contraband and his possessions inventoried. The inmate should be provided clothing and supplies and assigned housing.

The officer should determine the security level of the inmate, whether the inmate is a member of a security threat group (gang), and whether the inmate needs protection from any other inmates. Medical, mental health, education, and substance abuse testing should be conducted. The inmate should be interviewed and his file reviewed to determine case management strategy.

Pre-service and in-service training

Training is a structured activity designed to achieve specific learning objective(s). It may be classroom-based on involve pen and paper tests, it may involve hands-on training, at the job site, or it may include a physical component, such as firearms or self-defense training.

Before a corrections officer begins duty, he will go through "pre-service" training. Pre-service training covers the philosophy, methods, and techniques of corrections. It usually lasts several weeks and covers the basic functions of the corrections officer's job.

In-service training, on the other hand, is conducted after the officer has begun duty. Most employers require a certain amount of in-service training each year. In-service training may provide a review of basic skills and facility policies, introduce new procedures, or it may focus on a special area, such as working with inmates with special needs.

Occupational stress

Corrections officers work under stressful conditions. This stress comes not only from the challenges of working with inmates but also from the institution itself and from the general population, which tends to negatively stereotype corrections officers. Occupational stress can cause mental and physical damages and can lead to burnout – a feeling of hopelessness, frustration, and detachment.

Management must encourage personal and professional development. A stress awareness program can help officers manage their stress by acknowledging their feelings and learning visualization and breathing exercises. Another important strategy is career development. Corrections officers frequently cite a lack of professional opportunities as a source of job stress. Career development involves identifying the officer's desired career path in corrections and mapping out a plan for the officer to achieve his objectives. The plan will identify the sequence of steps the officer must take as well as any educational or licensure requirements.

Sexual harassment

Sexual harassment occurs when sexual behavior is proposed as a condition of employment, or if one worker's sexual conduct intrudes into the lives of other workers. Anytime that the sexual conduct of one person has an adverse effect on the ability of another person to do his or her job, sexual harassment has occurred. Anytime sexual advances contribute to a hostile work environment, this can be defined as sexual harassment.

There are two types of sexual harassment. With *quid pro quo harassment*, the employee is expect to accept the harassment in return for a job benefit, such as a promotion, a raise, or merely retaining his or her job. Quid pro quo harassment is, by definition, committed by a supervisor or other member of management who has the ability to confer or withhold the job benefit.

Hostile environment harassment occurs when the workplace is so contaminated with sexual images, comments, and innuendoes as to interfere with the employee's ability to do her work. Supervisors, co-workers, and even visitors and inmates can create a hostile environment. However, a single incident of harassment does not create a hostile environment unless the harassment is severe. Moreover, the employee has an obligation to report hostile environment harassment to provide management an opportunity to address the situation.

Security classifications

Institutions are categorized based on the security level of inmate they can serve. The basic levels of facility security are the same as for inmate classifications: minimum, medium, and maximum. In addition, some prison systems recognize a level called "close security," which is between maximum and medium security, and almost all systems have a pre-release level. There are also a growing number of facilities, or units within facilities, that are designated as "supermax." There are no universal definitions of these terms. What constitutes "maximum security" in one jurisdiction may be "medium security" in another jurisdiction.

The federal Bureau of Prisons uses the terms "low security" interchangeably with "minimum security," and refers to these facilities as "camps." In addition, the BOP operates "administrative facilities," which are the rough equivalent of supermax prisons.

Minimum-security facilities – sometimes called Level II – are the next-to-lowest security level. They are used for inmates who are not considered to pose a threat of violence or escape. They are typically white-collar criminals or those with only a short time remaining on their sentences. Housing is dormitory style with communal sanitary facilities. Prisoners may move freely throughout the facility and, in some cases, may leave the campus during the day on release programs. Prisoners in these facilities are often used as labor in the higher security facilities.

Minimum security facilities may be surrounded by a fence, instead of a wall. Some have a clearly-marked perimeter instead of a fence. Guards usually are not armed.

Medium-security facilities – sometimes called Level III – usually house nonviolent offenders. Housing is typically dormitory-style, but some facilities may have cells. Sanitary facilities are usually communal. Inmates are generally locked in their sleeping quarters for 10 to 12 hours per day, but are allowed to leave their cells to eat and for recreation, education, and counseling purposes. Inmates are allowed some freedom of movement within the facility, often through a pass system. Medium-security facilities often have a small number of single-cell units that are used for discipline, i.e., solitary confinement. The facility itself is typically surrounded by one or two walls, with armed guards posted at watch towers. The walls usually have razor wire on top to prevent escape. Internal security may be managed through electronic surveillance.

Maximum-security facilities: Maximum-security facilities – sometimes called Level V – have a very high level of security, both in terms of individual inmate housing and perimeter controls. These facilities are used for inmates who present the highest risk to society, staff, and other inmates. Cells are typically single or double occupancy, with sanitary facilities inside the cell to reduce the need to move

- 38 -

inmates. Inmates are usually locked in their cells for 23 hours per day. Inmates must be escorted by officers when moving throughout the facility.

As for perimeter control, maximum-security facilities are usually continuously patrolled by armed guards. They typically have double or even triple walls, including razor wire and/or electrical fencing with a fatal level of voltage.

Supermax facilities: Supermax is the highest security level and is used for inmates who have had discipline problems in other facilities, inmates who are known threats, and high-profile inmates. Confinement in a supermax facility is similar to solitary confinement, with single-occupancy cells and in-cell sanitary facilities. Inmates are allowed out of their cells for one hour each day to exercise in a small, cement pen. All staff-to-inmate interaction, including religious services, is done through the cell bars. Full restraint is used for any movement of the inmate, internal or external.

The supermax facility may contain unusual security measures. Cells at the BOP's supermax facility in Florence, Colorado are almost soundproof and drainpipes are routed to a central damping area, to prevent communication between inmates. No physical contact is permitted with visitors – inmates speak with visitors over the telephone. Access to the facility is through a tunnel.

Security measures

Higher security prisons have protected perimeters and limited points of entry. Perimeters are protected by physical barriers, namely two to three fences or walls spaced 20 to 30 feet apart. Razor wire may be used on top of or between the walls. Armed guards monitor the perimeter from towers set at regular intervals. The facility may also use mobile patrols –guards who patrol the outside of the perimeter by motorized vehicle.

In addition, higher security prisons have a limited number of entrances for vehicles and personnel, usually no more than one or two, as well as gates between the administrative areas and the inmate areas of the institution. Finally, all vehicles that enter or leave the premises are subjected to inspection, including inspection of the undercarriage of the vehicle.

"Sally ports"

A sally port is a double-gated entrance to a facility. The gates are operated by a guard in a secure area, using remote controls. Only one gate is opened at a time, allowing the person or vehicle to enter as far as the second gate. The first gate is then closed. In this way, the visitor is held between the gates while the person and/or vehicle is searched and authorization is confirmed. After the inspection is complete, the second gate is opened and the visitor is allowed to enter the facility. Because the first gate was closed after the visitor, there is no opening through which inmates can escape. If any problems arise while the visitor is held in between the two gates, the guard can lock down both gates and hold the visitor securely.

Control centers and safety vestibules

Both a control center and a safety vestibule are designed to provide physical barriers inside of a corrections facility. A control center is a secure, enclosed area that houses critical controls, such as fire alarms, and gate and door controls. The control center may also house keys to restricted areas.

A safety vestibule, on the other hand, is the equivalent of an internal sally port. It is an enclosed area, access to which is controlled by a series of two doors or gates, usually operated by remote control. The doors or gates are used to slow down traffic between the two areas connected by the vestibule and to ensure that only authorized persons move between those two areas.

- 40 -

Writ of detainer

A writ is an order issued by a court or an administrative body. A writ of detainer is similar to an arrest warrant in that it directs an institution to hold a person. A law enforcement agency may issue a writ of detainer to a corrections institution asking the institution to hold an inmate until the inmate can be transferred to the custody of the agency. An agency may also issue a writ of detainer to direct the institution to notify the agency if the person is about to be released. For this reason, an institution may have a practice or procedure of checking for writs of detainer before releasing an inmate from the institution. A writ of detainer is different from an arrest warrant because the person against whom it is directed is already in custody.

Felonies and misdemeanors

Both felonies and misdemeanors are criminal offenses, but felonies are more serious than misdemeanors. In most states, felonies are punishable by imprisonment for more than one year. Violent crimes are crimes against the person, such as murder and assault with bodily injury; they are usually felonies. Serious drug crimes and property crimes (theft and burglary) may also be felonies. Everything that is not a felony is a misdemeanor.

In most states, a person who has been convicted of a felony is "disenfranchised," meaning that the person loses the right to vote. In all but two states, convicted felons who are currently in prison are not allowed to vote. Some states reinstate voting rights after the convicted felon has completed his or her sentence. Other states provide that convicted felons lose the right to vote permanently.

Probation and parole

Both probation and parole involve supervised release of an offender. Probation is imposed after the offender is convicted, but before he is incarcerated. The offender is sentenced, but the sentence is suspended while the offender is put on probation. Parole is imposed after the offender has been incarcerated, but before the offender has completed his sentence.

In either case, the offender must meet regularly with an official to review his status. If the offender violates certain conditions, the offender is sent to prison, in the case of probation, or is returned to prison, in the case of parole. Probation and parole, along with other programs for supervision of inmates who are not currently incarcerated, are referred to as "community corrections."

Nolle prosequi and *nolo contendere*

Nolle prosequi – commonly referred to as "nol-pros" – is a decision by the prosecutor not to pursue a criminal charge. The benefit of a nol-pros is it does not count as a prosecution for double jeopardy purposes. Accordingly, a prosecutor may drop charges to avoid the bar of double jeopardy.

Nolo contendere – commonly referred to as "nolo" or "no contest" – is a decision by the accused not to fight the charges. The accused does not admit guilt by pleading guilty. He is, however, subject to the full range of sentencing. Moreover, in some states the accused is barred from appealing the sentence. The benefit of a nolo plea is that it is not an admission of guilt for civil purposes, such as where the victim sues the accused for money damages.

Adjudication

The term adjudication refers to a court's determination on the charges in a criminal case. There are many types of adjudications. A *conviction* is a determination that the accused is guilty of the crime. An *acquittal* is a determination that the accused is not guilty. A *dismissal* occurs either as a result of a *nolle prosequi* or because the court determines that there is insufficient evidence to even hold the accused over for trial. Most states use different terms for the adjudication of minors. A juvenile who is found to have committed a crime may be adjudicated a "delinquent." or "in need of supervision."

Deferred adjudication is a suspension of charges. As with probation, the accused must comply with certain conditions. If the accused completes the period of deferred adjudication without incident, the charges are dropped.

Expunction and deferred adjudication

Deferred adjudication is a suspension of charges before conviction. The accused must comply with a set of conditions, such as not incurring any more criminal charges for a period of time. If the accused violates the conditions, the charges are prosecuted. The benefit of deferred adjudication is that successful completion of the conditions results in no record of a conviction. However, the arrest may remain on the record of the accused.

Expunction – also called expungement – is the removal of criminal charges after an adjudication other than guilt. For example, an expunction may be available after a *nolle prosequi* dismissal of the charges. In some cases, such as with minors, an expunction may be available after the sentence has been served, if the accused

- 43 -

maintains a clean criminal record for an extended period of time. A court order is usually required for an expunction.

Sentencing guidelines

The federal government and most states have adopted guidelines for judges to use in setting sentences. Typically, sentencing guidelines determine punishment based on the type of crime and the offender's criminal record. A judge may "depart" from the prescribed sentence only if the judge finds that mitigating or aggravating factors exist.

The intention of adopting guidelines was to provide consistency throughout a state, so that offenders who committed similar crimes were not punished more harshly by a judge in one part of a state and less harshly by a judge in another part of the state. The guidelines were also intended to address concerns about discrimination based on race, gender, and other protected characteristics, by providing an objective system for determining sentences.

Determinate and indeterminate sentences

A determinate sentence is a sentence for a set period of time. Officials have no discretion to reduce a determinate sentence for good behavior or due to mitigating factors. An example of a determinate sentence is a "three strikes" law that requires life imprisonment, without possibility of parole, after a third felony conviction. An indeterminate sentence consists of a maximum period of incarceration, with the possibility of parole or other early release. Some sentences are a combination between determinate and indeterminate. An example would be a requirement that an inmate serve a minimum number of years of his sentence, after which the inmate may be eligible for early release. Corrections officials often complain that determinate sentencing removes any incentive an inmate may have for good behavior, because the inmate cannot influence the length of his incarceration.

Concurrent and consecutive sentences

Concurrent sentences are sentences that an inmate is allowed to serve at the same time. The inmate's total sentence is the length of the longest sentence. Concurrent sentences may be imposed where the offender is sentenced for more than one crime arising out of the same incident. For example, a drunk driver who kills a pedestrian may be convicted of vehicular manslaughter, driving under the influence, and speeding, but may be allowed to serve the sentences for all three convictions simultaneously.

Consecutive sentences are sentences that the inmate must serve one after the other. The inmate's total sentence is the sum of all of the sentences added together. Consecutive sentences may be imposed where there is one criminal incident, but several victims. For example, an offender who murders three persons in a drive-by shooting may be convicted on three counts of murder and required to serve three sentences, consecutively.

Inmate classification

Inmate classification, or inmate custody category, refers to the custody requirements for an inmate based on his criminal record, number of years left on his sentence, behavior toward staff and other inmates, association with a security threat group (gang), history of escape attempts, and possible threats from others. In most states, classification of inmates is done according to objective guidelines.

Most institutions classify inmates as minimum, medium, and maximum security. Some institutions recognize a fourth custody level, "close custody," for inmates who are considered to pose a risk of violence toward others. An inmate's classification determines the type of facility in which he is confined, housing within the facility, and the programs he can participate in. For example, an inmate classified as maximum security will generally be sent to a maximum-security institution.

Protective custody

There are two types of protective custody in prisons. The first is the protected custody extended to federal witnesses who are incarcerated. This type of protective custody is similar to a regular witness protection program in that the goal is to protect the individual so he or she can provide testimony against another person. A federal prison may have an entire unit devoted to this type of custody. Inmates in federal witness protection generally have less restrictions and more privileges than they would experience under other levels of security.

The second type of protective custody is that given to inmates who have been threatened or harassed by other inmates. This type of custody is more restrictive because the goal is to protect the inmate from others.

"Good time"

"Good time" refers to credits an inmate may earn through good behavior while in prison. Good time provides an incentive for the inmate to behave well in prison. The credits shorten the time until the inmate is eligible for parole.

Not all inmates are eligible for good time. Inmates who commit certain offenses are not eligible. In some jurisdictions, most notably those with "three strikes" rules, repeat offenders are not eligible for good time. Some jurisdictions – those with determinate sentencing – do not recognize any good time.

Critics of good time complain that the reduction in time served is misleading to jurors who do the sentencing. A well-behaved inmate might serve one-third of his sentence. This has led to "truth in sentencing" laws, which require that jurors be informed of the effect of good time at the time they are deciding the sentence.

Honor blocks

An honor block is a block of cells for inmates who have maintained good behavior for a specified period of time. There may be other requirements for transfer to the honor block, such as having a prison job.

Inmates in honor blocks usually receive more privileges, such as better visitation and more freedom of movement. They may also have better facilities, such as larger cells and hot tap water inside the cell.

Placement in the honor block must be earned through good behavior and specifically requested by the inmate. The inmate must continue to earn the placement while in the honor block. Any disciplinary infraction can result return to a regular cell block.

A "count"

A "count" is a full head count of all inmates in a facility or in a particular unit of a facility. Counts are taken several times a day, usually at specified times. Typically, inmates are required to return to their cells for the count. An accurate count helps the facility ensure that no inmate has escaped or is in an unauthorized location. If an inmate does escape, his absence will be discovered by the next count. The count also gives officers an opportunity to see every inmate regularly to make sure that no inmate's physical status has changed dramatically. A formal count involves the entire facility. In addition, officers conduct informal counts at the beginning and end of each shift.

Constitutional rights of inmates

Convicted prisoners do not lose all of their constitutional rights. They do, however, lose some. They lose those rights that are inconsistent with incarceration, such as the right to liberty. In addition, they are not protected from prison regulations that have a "rational relationship" to legitimate penological interests. Legitimate penological interests include rehabilitation, deterrence of crime, and institutional security. If the prison can demonstrate a rational relationship between an institutional rule and these interests, the rule will be upheld, even if it impinges on an inmate's constitutional rights. Pretrial detainees – those who are in jail awaiting trial – also have the right not to be punished, because they have not yet been found guilty.

The First Amendment

The First Amendment guarantees freedom of expression. Freedom of expression encompasses four basic liberties: freedom of speech, religion, press, and assembly. Freedom of speech is the right to express one's views, as well as the right to receive the views of others. Freedom of religion is the right to practice one's own religious beliefs. Freedom of the press is the right of the media to publish as well as the right of citizens to communicate information to the media that is of public interest. Freedom of assembly – also called freedom of association – is the right of an individual to join others in a group and the right to associate with another person.

The First Amendment to the Constitution states that no law should be allowed to infringe on the freedoms of religion, speech, press, peaceable assembly, and petition. In order to retain the security of a correctional facility, it is often necessary to suspend First Amendment rights. Outside of correctional institutions, it must be demonstrated that the exercise of these rights is a "clear and present danger" before they can be curtailed. Correctional facilities have a much lower burden of proof in cases regarding the suspension of First Amendment rights.

Inmate mail: Courts divide inmate mail into two categories for First Amendment analysis: nonlegal and legal. As to nonlegal mail, courts distinguish between mere inspection, to search for contraband, and censorship, the actual withholding of mail. Prisons have broad discretion to inspect nonlegal inmate mail, if the search is necessary to serve legitimate penological interests. Censorship of nonlegal mail, on the other hand, raises free speech issues. The institution must demonstrate how censorship furthers legitimate penological interests. In addition, the institution must notify the inmate and the author of the censorship and provide an opportunity for review. Legal mail, by contrast, is absolutely protected. Mail between inmates and courts, attorneys, or their representatives may not be opened and searched for contraband unless the inmate is present.

Although there is not a specific law governing inbound and outbound mail of inmates, Supreme Court cases have demonstrated that certain material, such as racist or pornographic material, can be blocked from entry into a correctional facility. However, any time mail is blocked the prisoner must be notified and given a chance to protest. A prisoner's legal mail or mail from the media cannot be read by unauthorized individuals, though it must be opened in the presence of the prisoner and searched for contraband. Outbound mail is much less restricted, and is usually opened only when it is believed to contain information that threatens security or rehabilitation.

Inmate religious beliefs: The First Amendment protects inmates in their religious beliefs. This means, first, that a prison cannot force inmates to practice a particular religion or, for that matter, to practice any religion at all. Second, the prison cannot discriminate against or disparage an inmate for following his or her religious beliefs.

The more difficult question is the extent to which prisons must accommodate religious practices. Generally, courts require prisons to reasonably accommodate religious practices that do not conflict with legitimate penological interests. For example, a prison may have to accommodate the dietary restrictions of a Jewish inmate, but not the hair-length restrictions of a Native American inmate if the prison already restricted inmate hair length for security and health reasons.

Inmate access to the media: An institution may restrict media access to inmates if the restriction meets the four parts of the *Turner* test. If an institution permits media access, it may restrict the conditions of the access, such as barring face-to-face interviews.

There are two limits on the above. First, the restrictions may not be an "exaggerated response" to prison concerns. Second, the restrictions may not be based on the content of the inmate's speech. For example, a prison may not permit media access to inmates with positive comments about the institution, while restricting access to inmates with complaints.

Finally, the press does not have a right of access to any individual inmate. Such access would be greater than the media's right of access to citizens in the general population, and there is no basis for such greater access.

Inmate visitation: Inmate visitation involves the First Amendment right to freedom of association. The most significant outside relationships for most inmates are those with family and other visitors. Prison restrictions on contact visits have been upheld as constitutional. In the 2003 case of *Overton v. Bazzetta*, the Supreme Court upheld restrictions on the number and type of non-contact visits inmates could receive under Michigan rules. These rules limited visits by minors to the children and grandchildren of the inmate. Former inmates could visit only if related to the inmate. An inmate with two or more substance abuse violations could only have visits from lawyers and clergy. The court held that all of these restrictions were legitimate.

Inmate access to books, newspapers, magazines, and similar material: Citizens in the general population have a First Amendment right of access to printed media. Inmates have that same right, but it can be curtailed by the institution if the *Turner* test is satisfied. The Supreme Court recently held that a prison could cut off inmate access to secular (non-religious) newspapers and periodicals for inmates who were assigned to a high-security unit. Prison officials justified the rule on the ground that it provided an incentive for inmates to comply with prison rules.

Most prisons ban hard-core pornography, child pornography, sadomasochistic pornography, literature from hate groups, and weapons manuals, all on the ground that they create security threats. Courts will generally defer to prison officials' judgment on these matters. Similarly, the Supreme Court upheld a ban on hardback books not mailed directly from the publisher. The prison argued that the rule addressed a security threat.

The Fourth Amendment

The Fourth Amendment protects citizens against unreasonable searches and seizures by the government. The three elements of a Fourth Amendment claim are: (1) reasonableness; (2) justification; and (3) expectation of privacy.

Reasonableness: The key to any Fourth Amendment claim is whether the government's actions were "reasonable." Courts will look at whether a search was "justified at its inception," as opposed to being justified because

- 51 -

contraband was in fact located, and reasonable in the way that the search is conducted.

As to privacy, courts will look at whether the individual has a reasonable expectation of privacy in the area searched, whether that is the individual's body, his clothing, his possessions, or his living space. Even if an individual has a reasonable expectation of privacy, the individual can waive his rights by consenting to the search. Thus, a frequent question in privacy cases is whether the individual voluntarily consented. Consent to premises by a third party, such as a cellmate, is effective if that party had common authority of the premises.

Searches: Inmates have little Fourth Amendment protection. Prison officials are free to search an inmate's possessions and living quarters, with or without reasonable cause. Random, "shake down" searches have been upheld by the courts. The Supreme Court has concluded that an inmate has no reasonable expectation of privacy in his cell or its contents. However, any searches must be conducted pursuant to a valid prison regulation and may not be for purposes of harassment or wanton destruction of the inmate's property.

The rules for inspection of an inmate's person are more restrictive. Generally, the greater the intrusive of the search, the greater the reason must be for conducting the search. A visual search of a fully clothed inmate is minimally invasive and so requires little or no justification. On the other hand, a body cavity search must in most cases be based on reasonable suspicion that the inmate is hiding contraband.

In order for an officer's suspicion to be considered reasonable by a court, it must be based on a combination of fact and professional judgment. In other words, there must be a specific fact that arouses the suspicion, and the suspicion must be focused on a particular individual or group rather than on the prison population as a whole.

The courts have rules that anonymous tips do not constitute a fact that can justify invasive searches. Whenever a full body search or strip search is performed, the rationale must be documented.

Cross-gender searches: Courts balance the intrusiveness of the search against the justification for the search, and then determine whether the gender of the officer is a factor. They also factor in female officers' equal employment rights.

Visual: Visual inspection of a fully-clothed inmate is permissible by either gender of officer. A female officer may observe male inmates who are not clothed – such as in the shower – but it is less clear whether a male officer may observe female inmates under the same situations.

Pat-down searches: Pat down searches of fully-clothed inmates, conducted pursuant to established rules and procedures, are usually permissible by either gender, even if the anal and genital area is involved.

Strip/body cavity searches: Strip searches and body cavity searches are usually permitted where the inmate is male and the officer is female. Courts are hesitant to these intrusive searches of female inmates by male officers, however.

The courts have sanctioned both males and females to act as prison guards over both male and female prison populations. However, it is becoming increasingly clear that female prisoners have greater privacy needs. Most female prisoners are unwilling to be naked in front of male prison guards, though male prisoners are not unwilling to be naked in front of female guards. Searches also provide opportunity for conflict. Searches should only be performed by prisoners of the same sex unless there is an emergency.

The Fifth Amendment

The three elements of the Fifth Amendment that arise in the corrections context are the prohibitions against double jeopardy, self-incrimination, and punishment without due process of law.

Double jeopardy is putting a defendant "in jeopardy" more than once for the same offense. This may include a second prosecution for the same offense, after either acquittal or conviction. It may also encompass multiple punishments for the same offense. The two most common double jeopardy claims are prison discipline and correction of administrative mistakes.

The first situation arises when an inmate who commits an offense while in prison faces criminal charges and administrative discipline for the offense. Inmates argue that this violates the double jeopardy clause because they are being punished twice for the same offense. Courts reject these claims because the double jeopardy clause applies only to criminal punishments. Institutional discipline is not the same as criminal punishment.

The second situation arises when the institution or criminal justice system makes a mistake regarding an inmate, such as erroneously releasing an inmate early, then reincarcerating him when the mistake is discovered. Other examples are mistakes in calculating sentences or good time. Courts have held that correction of clerical mistakes is not a criminal prosecution or punishment.

Self-incrimination, another element of the Fifth Amendment, is the privilege not to have to testify against oneself if the testimony might result in criminal sanctions, including fines and other penalties. This privilege is not available if the government grants the witness immunity from prosecution. The due process clause of the Fifth

Amendment prohibits the government from depriving a person of life, liberty, or property without due process of law.

Treatment programs:

An inmate's participation in a treatment program violates the Fifth Amendment if: (1) the inmate's case is on appeal; and (2) the inmate's participation is coerced.

Inmates complain that participation in certain treatment programs, such as for sex offenders, constitutes an admission of guilt. This is important only if an inmate is appealing his conviction. Once all appeals have been exhausted, the issue of self-incrimination is moot.

In *McKune v. Lile*, the Supreme Court held that a prison does not violate the Fifth Amendment by removing certain incentives – such as preferred housing – if an inmate refuses participation, even if there are negative consequences to the inmate. This is because the Fifth Amendment does not prohibit all self-incrimination, just *compelled* self-incrimination. Therefore, an institution may offer incentives to participate. An institution cannot coerce or force an inmate to participate.

Miranda warnings

An inmate is entitled to a *Miranda* warning if: (1) he is being interrogated; (2) about a potential criminal matter. In *Miranda v. Arizona*, the Supreme Court held that, due to the coercive nature of custodial interrogation, a suspect must be informed of his rights. Inmates are in a custodial situation, but an inmate is not entitled to a *Miranda* warning every time he is questioned about his conduct.

Courts look at the conditions of the confession. Admissions to corrections staff under ordinary prison conditions are not "interrogations." If the inmate is separated from the rest of the population and interviewed under coercive conditions not normally experienced in prison, a *Miranda* warning may be required. Similarly, confessions to cellmate informants, even if they are undercover officers, are admissible if they are not coerced. Finally, a *Miranda* warning is not required for disciplinary actions, only criminal charges.

The Sixth Amendment

There are three elements of the right to effective assistance of counsel in the Sixth Amendment. The three elements are: (1) access; (2) privacy; (3) and effective assistance.

- <u>Access</u>: An inmate has a right of access to counsel. This right is not limited to assistance with criminal charges. It encompasses any legal counseling.
- <u>Privacy</u>: An inmate has a right to privacy of communication with counsel. As a general rule, prison staff may not read an inmate's correspondence with his attorney or listen to his conversations with his attorney. Incidental monitoring may not violate the Sixth Amendment if information is not shared with the prosecution. Systematic monitoring would violate the Sixth Amendment, even if information is not shared with the prosecution, because of the chilling (self-censoring) effect it could have on inmate-counsel communications.
- <u>Effective Assistance</u>: For effective assistance of counsel, the inmate and attorney must be permitted to form a relationship. Accordingly, the prison may not arbitrarily limit the inmate's access to legal counsel.

The Eighth Amendment

The Eighth Amendment prohibits cruel and unusual punishment. The courts system is in a continuous process of determining what constitutes cruel and unusual punishment. Some of the basic guidelines suggest that a punishment can be considered cruel and unusual if it: shocks the conscience of the court; violates the evolving standards of decency of a civilized society; is disproportionate to the offense; and entails the wanton and unnecessary infliction of pain. To prevail on a claim that the conditions of confinement violate this prohibition, an inmate must demonstrate that: (1) prison officials were deliberately indifferent to: (2) unconstitutional conditions of confinement.

As to conditions of confinement, inmates are entitled to "the minimum civilized measure of life's necessities." This includes essential food, medical care, and sanitation, as well as protection from harm by other inmates and from excessive force. In evaluating the conditions of confinement, courts will look at individual factors alone and in combination, to determine the "totality of circumstances." Overcrowding is not a violation in itself, but the effects of overcrowding on health, sanitation, and safety may be a violation due to their combined impact.

The courts system may rule on the conditions of confinement in cases where the conditions are thought to lack safety or some other basic human need. The human needs that must be provided in any correctional setting are as follows: adequate exercise; nutritional diet; clothing appropriate to the climate conditions of the institution; shelter (including plumbing, ventilation; and climate control); sanitation; medical care; and reasonable safety.

Excessive force: Force is excessive if it was not justified by a legitimate penological purpose or if it was disproportionate to the purpose. Although officials may use force to restore and maintain discipline, they may not use it maliciously and sadistically.

<u>Justified</u>: In determining whether force was justified, courts look at the extent of the risk to inmates and staff. They also look at whether efforts were made to reduce the risk through other methods before using force. Sexual contact between a prison official and an inmate is never justified, even if it was "consensual," because of the imbalance of power.

<u>Proportionate</u>: In determining whether force was proportionate, courts look at the immediacy and seriousness of the threat. Force used after the threat has passed is rarely justified. Courts will also consider the extent of the inmate's injuries. An inmate need not show a serious or permanent physical injury, however.

There are three types of records that are especially important in determining whether excessive force has been used:

- Videotapes: perhaps the most effective way of describing the situation to a judge or jury
- Incident reports: detailed summaries composed after any situation in which force was required; these reports should include a description of the force used as well as the justification for the force
- Medical records: in most cases, inmates should be examined after force has been used; inmates should be treated for any injuries sustained as a result of force

A correctional officer should be sure to abide by any institutional, state, or federal policies regarding the use of force. Force should only be used in situations where all other means have been exhausted, and should never be considered an appropriate means of punishment. Any time force is used, it must be documented and submitted for review by supervisors. Finally, if a court is required to examine the use of force, it will do so from the point of view of the correctional officer.

Liability: The two conditions under which an officer may be liable for the excessive force of another officer are: (1) failure to intervene; or (2) supervisor liability.

- <u>Failure to Intervene</u>: An officer is liable for the excessive force of another if the officer was present when the force was being used and he failed to intervene to stop it. In such cases, courts apply the "deliberate indifference" standard, rather than "malicious and sadistic."

- <u>Supervisory Liability</u>: A supervisor is liable for the excessive force of a subordinate if the supervisor was deliberately indifferent to the risk of a violation. This may arise, for example, where excessive force is regularly used in an institution, with the knowledge of a supervisor, the supervisor fails to take corrective action, and an inmate is seriously injured.

Failure to protect an inmate from another inmate: The four elements of a claim of this nature are:

- <u>Substantial Risk of Serious Harm</u>: A strong likelihood, rather than a mere possibility, that the inmate would suffer serious harm. There is no bright line rule for when an injury is "serious," but minor injuries probably are not enough.

- <u>Official Knew of Risk</u>: The official must have known there was risk to the specific inmate, to a group to which the inmate belong, or within the prison in general. Knowledge may arise because the official was specifically told of the risk or because the risk was obvious.

- <u>Unreasonable Failure to Respond</u>: The official must have failed to reasonably respond to the risk. This does not mean the official must eliminate the risk in every case, just that the official made good faith efforts to address the risk.

- <u>Causation</u>: There must be a connection between the official's failure to respond and the assault.

Failure-to-protect claims: The six most common failure-to-protect claims are:

- Unusually vulnerable inmates: Officials failed to take reasonable steps to protect an inmate who was a likely target of assault. Likely targets include informants, the mentally ill, inmates who are smaller, and those known as homosexuals.

- Unusually dangerous inmates: Officials failed to properly classify and isolate unusually dangerous inmates, especially inmates with a history of violence behind bars.

- Attacker threatened victim: Officials failed to reasonably protect an inmate who was threatened.

- Failure to intervene: Officials witnessed an attack, but failed to take reasonable steps to stop it. Officials need not, however, endanger their own safety.

- Overcrowding and Understaffing: These conditions do not, alone, violate the constitution. If, however, they lead to more violence, then they may give rise to a failure- to-protect claim.

"Deliberate indifference"

Occasionally, a prisoner will claim that his or her rights under the Eighth Amendment have been violated by incompetent or negligent medical care or safety care. For instance, an officer can be charged with deliberate indifference if he or she does not allow a prisoner to visit a doctor. The medical staff can be held responsible if the care they provide is inadequate or indifferent to serious medical needs. Another scenario in which an institution or individual can be charged with negligence or deliberate indifference is when a preexisting medical condition is not considered when establishing a prisoner's living conditions.

A prison official displays deliberate indifference if he had actual knowledge of a serious risk of substantial injury and unreasonably failed to take action to correct the problem.

- Actual knowledge: The official must have had actual knowledge of the conditions and that the conditions posed a substantial risk of serious injury to inmates. Knowledge can be inferred if the conditions are longstanding, pervasive, well-documented, or expressly noted. An inmate need not show an intent to harm, but must show more than mere negligence.

- Unreasonable failure to act: A prison official must make a good faith effort to investigate the problem and fix it. In deciding whether an official's response was reasonable, courts look at the information he possessed at the time, the practical limitations of his position, and any alternative courses of action that would have been apparent to an official in his position. Cost is not a defense.

The Fourteenth Amendment

The Fourteenth Amendment to the Constitution declares that the state should not "deprive any person of life, liberty, or property without due process of law." Also, it declares that no state should "deny to any person within its jurisdiction the equal protection of the laws." In other words, a person must be given due process before they are incarcerated. Also, no person should be denied the rights to defend themselves accorded by law. Although this due process law is directed at the state governments, there is a similar provision applying to the federal government in the Fifth Amendment.

The steps of due process when a serious sanction is threatened are as follows:
- There is a hearing at which the inmate has a right to be present.
- The inmate is given notice of the charges against him or her at least 24 hours before the hearing.

- The inmate is given the opportunity to call witnesses and present evidence on his or her own behalf.
- Although the inmate does not have a right to counsel, he or she does have a right to assistance if he or she is illiterate or otherwise prevented from preparing for the hearing.
- The inmate has the right to an impartial tribunal, excluding any individual who was involved in the alleged infraction
- The tribunal is required to record its findings, ruling, and rationale in writing.

Due process policies for disciplinary actions: court cases
- *Wolff v. McDonnell* (1974): a hearing is required when good time is forfeited due to misbehavior; also, a hearing is required when an inmate faces a term of segregation due to misbehavior
- *Sandin v. Conner* (1995): the terms of the *Wolff* decision were declared to be inapplicable to cases in which the disciplinary hearing would result in less than 30 days of segregation; unless the possible sanction imposes "atypical deprivation in relation to a normal prison life," a hearing is not necessary. Cases in which an inmate is medicated without consent or is committed to a mental institution require a due process hearing.

Procedural due process vs. substantive due process: Substantive due process is primarily concerned with the action that was taken, while procedural due process focuses on the way that action was performed. The courts insist that the corrections system abide by procedural due process so that the rights of prisoners will not be infringed upon. An issue of substantive due process concerns whether the institution has the right to do something in the first place, even when all of the necessary procedures are followed.

The Religious Land Use and Institutionalized Persons Act (RLUIPA)

Passed in 2000, the RLUIPA prohibits the government from imposing a substantial burden on the religious exercise of an inmate unless the burden: (1) furthers a "compelling governmental interest"; and (2) is the "least restrictive means" of furthering that interest.

The RLUIPA applies to individual acts burdening an inmate's religious exercise, and to rules of "general applicability" that have the effect, intentional or unintentional, of burdening an inmate's religious exercise.

The Act defines "religious exercise" broadly. An inmate need not be a member of a recognized religion. If the inmate is a member of a recognized religion, the exercise is protected even if it is not required by that religion.

In the 2005 case of *Cutter v. Wilkinson*, the Supreme Court held that the law is not unconstitutional, even if it results in more favorable treatment of inmate religious practices than other inmate practices.

The *Turner* test

The *Turner* test was developed by the Supreme Court in 1987 in the case of *Turner v. Safley*. This test is used to determine the constitutionality of prison regulations that infringe on an inmate's First Amendment rights. There are four parts to the test:

1. Whether there is a valid, rational connection between the regulation and a legitimate penological interest;
2. Whether the inmate has access to alternative means of exercising his rights;
3. Whether accommodation of the inmate's rights would have a "ripple effect" on the rest of the prison; and
4. Whether there is a ready alternative to the regulation that would accommodate the inmate's rights at minimal cost to penological interests.

In the *Turner* case, the Supreme Court upheld Ohio regulations restricting correspondence between inmates at different facilities. However, the court also struck down a requirement that the warden give permission for inmate marriages.

A Son of Sam law

A Son of Sam law prevents an inmate from profiting from his crimes through books and other media deals. These laws require the proceeds to go to the victim(s) of the crime. Approximately 40 states have adopted such laws.

In 1991, the Supreme Court struck down New York's Son of Sam law as overbroad and in violation of inmates' free speech rights under the First Amendment. The laws in many other states have either been struck down or are rarely invoked. As a result, the trend is away from mandatory forfeiture laws.

Crime victims may still access proceeds from media deals through civil lawsuits. As in the OJ Simpson case, the victim's family can always sue the inmate and collect any damages awarded from the inmate's assets. These assets would include proceeds from media deals.

Prison Rape Elimination Commission

Passed in 2003, the Prison Rape Elimination Act (PREA) created the Prison Rape Elimination Commission. The Commission's three duties are:

Study: The Commission is charged with conducting a two-year study of the policies and practices of corrections facilities for the prevention, detection, and punishment of prison rape regardless of whether committed by other inmates or by prison officials. The study must encompass the psychological and physical effects of prison rape, within the prison and in the community. <u>Standards</u>: The Commission must develop national standards, with the stated goal of making elimination of prison rape a top priority in every institution

<u>Report</u>:   At the end of its study, the Commission must report its findings and recommendations to Congress and the President.

Right to medical care

Inmates have a constitutional right to medical care that those in the outside world do not. The Supreme Court has held that failure to provide medical care can cause pain and suffering, which does not serve a penological purpose. Moreover, because they are incarcerated, inmates do not have the ability to seek out treatment on their own. They also may not be able to take recommended actions to prevent illness or injury, such as avoiding secondhand smoke, following a modified diet, or having regular dental cleanings.

The obligation to provide medical care may extend after release. Prison officials have a duty to continue to provide medical care after release until the offender can secure treatment on his own. For example, officials should provide an inmate who has a chronic condition with sufficient medicine to allow time for the offender to consult a provider to obtain a prescription.

Medical care claims

The four elements of a medical care claim are:
- <u>Serious medical need:</u> It must be life threatening, progressive (getting steadily worse), or very painful.

- Official knowledge: The official must be aware of the problem and any special threat the problem poses for the individual. For example, the common cold is not serious for the average adult, but can be very serious for someone with AIDS.
- Unreasonable failure to provide treatment: The official has a duty to take reasonable steps to obtain medical care. An official may not refuse to provide medically-adequate care because of cost. With infectious diseases, officials have a duty to obtain treatment to assist the individual *and* to prevent the spread of the infection to others.
- Causation: The inmate must show that the official's actions caused the inmate further injury, or unnecessary and wanton pain and suffering.

Medical care claims take three forms: (1) denial or delay of access to care; (3) inadequate care; or (3) interference with prescribed treatment.

- Denial or delay: An inmate may assert that an officer refused to allow him to see medical staff. An officer should not act as gatekeeper to medical staff unless he or she has been properly trained. Similarly, a member of the medical staff without specialized training should not deny an inmate access to a specialist. A delay in providing treatment may be unconstitutional if it is medically unjustified and clearly likely to make the inmate's condition worse.
- Inadequate care: Inmates do not have a right to choose their care, and medical malpractice (negligence) is not unconstitutional. However, grossly incompetent or inadequate care may violate inmates' rights.
- Interference: Once medical staff prescribes treatment, corrections staff may not interfere with the treatment.

Medical care lawsuits

To be liable for failure to provide medical care, a supervisor or government must have established or tolerated a deliberately indifferent policy or custom. Claims against supervisors and governments are called *systemic* claims, because they challenge the system, rather than the actions of individuals.

There are three common systemic claims for failure to provide medical care. The first is failure to provide adequate medical staff. This includes both quantity of staff – sufficient to treat inmates' medical needs -- and quality of staff – staff with appropriate qualifications. Second is failure to provide adequate medical facilities, either at the prison or at an outside location. The third claim is for failure to provide access to staff and facilities – essentially, failure to screen for short- and long-term medical problems and failure to have a workable sick call policy.

HIV and AIDS

An inmate is four times as likely as a person in the general population to be infected with HIV – human immunodeficiency virus. HIV is a virus that attacks the body's immune system. AIDS -- acquired immunodeficiency syndrome – is the condition that results when HIV weakens the immune system. The body is then vulnerable to opportunistic infections, such as pneumonia. A person infected with HIV may have no symptoms. A person with AIDS may be very sick.

HIV is spread through contact with blood, semen, vaginal fluid, or breast milk. It is not spread through contact with saliva or other casual contact. AIDS is a syndrome and is not itself contagious, although any infection may be contagious.

The progress of HIV can be slowed using protease inhibitors and other medications. AIDS is not itself treatable, but the infection may be treated or managed.

STDs

The most common sexually transmitted diseases (STDs) in the inmate population are syphilis, gonorrhea, chlamydia, and herpes. These infections may or may not be symptomatic. All are treatable. If they are not treated, however, they may have long-term impact on the inmate's fertility and may lead to more serious problems, such as cancer.

Inmates are a high-risk population for STDs, which are communicated through unprotected sexual activity and intravenous drug use. Infected inmates pose a risk to other inmates and to their partners upon release.

Health authorities see the inmate and detainee population as an opportunity to address the spread of STDs. Health authorities advocate routine screening and treatment of all arrestees, detainees, and convicts. They also advocate educational programs targeted at this risk group.

Tuberculosis

Prison inmates make up one of the five high-risk groups for tuberculosis (TB). TB is caused by a bacterium that attacks the lungs, throat, brain, and spine. Symptoms include fever, chills, coughing, and spitting up blood.

Most people with TB do not have symptoms. This is called *latent* TB. Latent TB is detected through a skin test. Latent TB is not contagious. TB that is symptomatic is called *active* TB. A person with active TB is highly contagious. The disease is spread through the air when the infected person coughs or sneezes. Because active TB is so contagious, an infected person must be isolated to prevent its spread to the rest of the population.

A person with latent TB can be treated to reduce the risk of an active infection. A person with active TB must be treated with antibiotics over a long period of time – 12 months or more.

Diabetes

An estimated 5% of inmates have diabetes. Diabetes is a disorder in the body's ability to metabolize food due to shortage of insulin, resulting in high blood sugar. Diabetes can damage the heart, kidney, and nerves, as well as the body's ability to heal itself. A person may develop diabetes as a child or as an adult.

Diabetes is not contagious. There is a strong genetic link, but some people who develop diabetes have no history of the disease in their family. Obesity is a risk factor for diabetes. Also, racial minorities, including Hispanics, African Americans, Asian Americans, and Pacific Islanders, are at higher risk for diabetes.

Diabetes is treated through the management of blood sugar levels. This may involve insulin injections, dietary restrictions, and an exercise program. Inmates with diabetes require long-term medical treatment, with an emphasis on self-management.

Epilepsy

Epilepsy is a seizure disorder, caused by uncontrolled electrical activity in the brain. Some seizures involve loss of consciousness, such as *grand mal* seizures. Other seizures have isolated effects. For example, a seizure may affect a person's sense of smell, sound, or taste. Most seizures last less than a minute.

Epilepsy has many causes. One common cause is a head or brain injury, such as from head trauma, a brain infection, or a brain tumor. Epilepsy is more common among inmates than among the general population. Experts speculate that inmates are more likely to have suffered head injuries. Some argue that epileptics are more like to be incarcerated because one type of the disorder – temporal lobe epilepsy – is associated with violent tendencies.

Epilepsy is treated with anti-seizure medication. Even with medication, some people will continue to have seizures, although their seizures may be less frequent or less severe.

Disability and the ADA

The Americans with Disabilities Act (ADA) outlaws discrimination on the basis of disability in employment, accommodations, telecommunications, transportation, and public facilities. Inmates and correctional officers alike enjoy the rights provided by this act. According to the ADA, a disability is any physical or mental impairment that would limit one or more life activities of a person. Individuals may also be considered disabled if they have a history of such impairment, or are regarded by others as having such an impairment.

The Americans with Disabilities Act (ADA) defines a disability as a mental or physical impairment that significantly limits a major life activity. A person is also considered disabled if he has a past record of disability or if someone perceives him as having a disability. Examples of disabilities include paralysis, blindness, deafness, clinical depression, and intellectual disability.

Disabled inmates have three basic rights. First, they are protected from discrimination. Prison officials cannot treat a disabled inmate differently because of his disability. Second, a disabled inmate is entitled to accessible facilities. Third, inmates are entitled to reasonable accommodation. Prison officials must include disabled inmates in prison programs and activities, unless that would fundamentally change a program or activity or cause the prison "undue hardship."

Pregnant inmates

The three basic rights of pregnant inmates are prenatal care, abortion, and medical care during labor. Prenatal care includes regular visits to a qualified provider, appropriate nutrition, and prenatal vitamins. Inmates have the right to an abortion until the fetus is capable of sustaining itself outside the womb, or if the life of the mother is in danger or in the case of rape. Federal funds may not be used to pay for an abortion, but they may be used to transport an inmate to an abortion provider.

Inmates have the right to medical care during labor. Due to recent controversy, most institutions will not shackle an inmate during labor unless there is a risk to staff, the baby, or the inmate herself. Inmates do not have the right to keep their babies with them after birth.

Suicide

The three groups of inmates that are at risk for suicide are the mentally ill, those withdrawing from drugs and alcohol, and those experiencing trauma from arrest or incarceration.

Suicide is the leading cause of death among inmates, with a suicide rate ten times higher than the general population. This has been attributed to three factors: a high rate of mental illness in the inmate population, enforced withdrawal from drugs and alcohol upon incarceration, and traumatic reaction to incarceration. A major difference between these three is in timing. Those who commit suicide in reaction to the trauma of arrest or incarceration are most likely to act within the first 24 hours. Those who commit suicide due to drug or alcohol withdrawal are most likely to act during the withdrawal period. The mentally ill, on the other hand, may act at any time, including months after arrest or incarceration.

The three most common claims in inmate suicide cases are: (1) failure to identify; (2) failure to monitor; and (3) failure to respond. Failure to identify includes failure to recognize that an inmate is a suicide risk. It also encompasses failure to communicate concerns to other officers, such as during shift changes, or to other institutions upon transfer. Failure to monitor includes failure to make rounds or failure of technological monitoring. Because of monitoring challenges, some institutions will use inmate monitors. Failure to respond includes the situation where staff is not trained to handle medical emergencies. These claims may also encompass failure to address vehicles for suicide. For example, removing implements from the inmate or blocking access to upper level "jumping off" points.

Viral hepatitis

The three most common types of viral hepatitis are A (HAV), B (HBV), and C (HCV). HAV is transmitted through the oral-fecal route. It is contracted through oral contact with feces, raw seafood, or contaminated food or water. HAV causes acute illness, but the body is capable of fighting the virus with appropriate medical treatment.

HBV is transmitted through blood, such as through transfusions (in third world countries), tattoos, or needle-sharing. It causes acute illness and, in some cases, chronic infection. Acute HBV is treated with bed rest and medication. Some cases of chronic respond to medication.

HCV is transmitted through blood, as with HBV. It causes chronic illness, but may be asymptomatic for 10 years or long. HCV causes tremendous damage and is usually fatal. Some cases of HCV respond to interferon. Vaccines are available for HAV and HBV, but not for HCV.

Asthma

Asthma is inflammation of the lungs. It makes breathing difficult and can even result in death. Symptoms include characteristic wheezing, coughing, and shortness of breath.

Asthma is not a contagious disease. It varies in severity. Some people have regular problems while others have only occasional problems. Asthma attacks are brought on by physical and environmental "triggers," usually allergies or respiratory illness. These triggers vary from person to person. For some, animal allergies will provoke an asthma attack. For others, cigarette smoke may be a trigger.

Asthma cannot be cured, but it can be managed through medications and environmental changes. Medications are classified as "relief" – used to treat symptoms during an attack – and preventative – used to reduce inflammation in the lungs. Relief medications are vital during an attack to prevent serious injury or death.

Drug abuse

The five classes of commonly abused drugs are: opiates and narcotics; central nervous system (CNS) stimulants; CNS depressants; hallucinogens; and tetrahydrocannabinols.

- Opiates and narcotics: These are painkillers that produce a euphoric effect. Opiates include heroin, opium, codeine, morphine, and oxycontin.

- CNS stimulants: These drugs produce a stimulating effect. Stimulants include cocaine and meth (methamphetamine), as well as nicotine and caffeine.

- CNS depressants: These drugs produce a soothing, anti-anxiety effect. Depressants include barbiturates (such as pentobarbital), benzodiazepine (such as Xanax and valium), and alcohol.

- Hallucinogens: These drugs produce hallucinations. They include LSD, PCP (angel dust), and mescaline.

- Tetrahydrocannabinols (THC): THC drugs produce a relaxing effect. They include marijuana and hashish.

Personality disorders

A personality disorder is a form of mental illness characterized by long-term behavioral and thought patterns. The Diagnostic and Statistical Manual of Mental Disorders, Fourth Edition, Text Revision (DSM-IV-TR) lists ten personality disorders, grouped into three classes. The three classes are:

- Class A: odd or eccentric. This group includes paranoid and schizoid personality types. (A schizoid personality is not the same as the mental illness schizophrenia.)

- Class B: dramatic, emotional, or erratic. This group includes borderline, antisocial, histrionic, and narcissistic personality types.

- Class C: anxious or fearful. This group includes the following: avoidant, dependent, and obsessive-compulsive personality types. (Obsessive-compulsive personality is not the same as obsessive-compulsive disorder.)

The DSM-IV-TR also lists behavioral patterns that are not classified as personality disorders, including passive-aggressiveness and self-defeating behavior.

Schizophrenia

Schizophrenia is a psychotic disorder characterized by disorganized thoughts, hallucinations, and impaired psychosocial skills. Management of schizophrenia requires a long-term, multidisciplinary treatment plan to address biological, interpersonal, cultural, and social needs.
Special considerations in the corrections setting include noncompliance, continuity of care, discharge planning, and psychosocial interventions. Noncompliance is a significant problem with schizophrenia. Patients may discontinue medication or fail to attend medical appointments, often with disastrous consequences. Along the same lines, continuity of care and discharge planning are important for inmates with schizophrenia. Detailed records and other communications are vital.

Finally, psychosocial interventions can minimize acute psychotic episodes and reinforce appropriate behaviors. Stressors for schizophrenics include periods of isolation, lack of structure, and stigmatization. It is important that schizophrenics have social interaction, to reality-test their perceptions. Schizophrenics respond well to positive reinforcement, such as privileges in the yard or priority in the dining hall.

Mental health treatment

Corrections officials must take reasonable steps to address the serious mental health issues of inmates. Unfortunately, mental health problems are very difficult to diagnose and there is no universally accepted definition of mental illness. If an official has knowledge of a serious problem, however, he may not be deliberately indifferent to the problem. Once a problem is identified, treatment should be made available to the inmate. Problems arise where the inmate refuses treatment, particularly medication.

The Supreme Court has held that an inmate may be forced to use anti-psychotic medication if: (1) the inmate presents a danger to himself or others; and (2) the medication is in his medical interest. Most institutions limit the administration of medication to court-ordered situations and emergencies. First, the institution will consider less restrictive alternatives. Even then, the medication will be administered in the lowest effective dose.

Elderly and terminally ill inmates

The average age of inmates is increasing faster than the overall prison population. The primary reason for this is longer sentences: truth-in-sentencing laws, determinate sentencing, and three-strikes laws. This means more inmates will live out their lives in prison.

There are two basic approaches for dealing with the end-of-life issues for elderly and other inmates: release or services. Most states and the Bureau of Prisons have mechanisms for early release of terminal of elderly patients. These include commutation or reduction of sentences, administrative leave, and furlough.

The other approach is to provide end-of-life services. Some states have units that are reserved for elderly inmates. Others provide for palliative (pain and disease management) care. A growing number of institutions are implementing hospice programs where the focus is on making the inmate comfortable.

Dental care

The inmate population is at high risk for dental problems. Most inmates come from "dentally illiterate" communities. Moreover, serious dental problems are associated with certain criminal activities, such as methamphetamine use.

Inmates have a constitutional right to treatment of cavities and similar problems that may become worse and cause undue pain. Inmates do not have a constitutional right to preventative dental care, such as routine cleanings, although many institutions provide such care. Similarly, they do not have the right to cosmetic procedures.

Inmates have the right to dental hygiene items, such as toothbrushes and toothpaste. Special toothbrushes and dental floss are manufactured for inmates that pose a lower security risk than conventional supplies. Health authorities view the period of incarceration as an opportunity. The National Commission on Correctional Health Care mandates dental education and oral-hygiene instruction for all inmates.

Bloodborne pathogens (BBP) programs

BBPs are diseases spread through contact with blood and other potentially infectious bodily fluids, including saliva, semen, mucous, and urine. A BBP program consists of three elements: (1) pre-exposure measures; (3) procedures to minimize exposure risk; and (4) post-exposure prophylaxis.

Pre-exposure measures consist of training and optional hepatitis B vaccination. Training must be provided upon hire and then repeated annually. The HBV vaccination must be offered to all employees, but an employee may decline. Procedures to minimize exposure risk include equipment and workplace practices.

Workplace practices include universal precautions, which call for treating all blood and other potentially infectious material as if it is infected. Equipment consists primarily of barriers, such as personal protective equipment (PPE). Post-exposure prophylaxis consists of baseline testing of the employee, such as testing for HIV, HBV, and TB, testing of the source individual, and follow-up testing and treatment of the employee.

Fee-for-service programs

A number of agencies charge inmates a co-payment, typically less than $10, for routine medical visits. The funds come from the inmate's trust account. The revenues produced by these programs are insignificant relative to the cost of providing inmate medical care. Proponents argue that these programs reduce abuse of sick call and teach fiscal responsibility.

The NCCHC opposes fee-for-service programs on the grounds that they impede access to care. Nonetheless, inmate lawsuits challenging these programs have not been successful.

Because the constitution guarantees medical care, fee-for-service programs cannot be used to deny adequate medical care. Services must be provided even if there are insufficient funds in an inmate's trust account. Moreover, NCCHC recommends that institutions apply the fee only to services initiated by the inmate. NCCHC recommends exceptions to the fee for emergencies (life threatening illnesses or injuries), routine screenings, follow-up visits, referrals to specialists, lab work, and x-rays.

Important terms

Segregation: the isolation of an individual prisoner. Prisoners may be separated from the rest of the prisoner population for three different reasons: for their own protection, for disciplinary reasons, and for basic administrative reasons.

Serious incident: any event involving a resident, employee, or visitor of a corrective facility that necessitates medical attention or threatens the security of the facility

Severe mental disturbance: any condition in which an individual cannot take care of him or herself, or in which the individual becomes a danger to him or herself or others

Shadow board: a special board used in corrective facility shops, on which the shape of every tool is outlined in its proper place on the board, so that it is easy to tell when a tool is missing.

Shakedowns: frequent and random searches of inmates, cells, and common areas; the purpose of a shakedown is to find contraband

Shivs/shanks: makeshift knives crafted out of materials commonly found in a correctional facility; common shiv/shank materials include toothbrushes, kitchen utensils, and shards of metal from lockers, bed frames, and from metal shops

Special diets: any system of nutrition that fulfills a therapeutic, religious, or dietotic purpose

Strip search: the examination of an inmate's naked body, bodily orifices, and clothing; strip searches are performed to detect weapons, contraband, and any other abnormalities

Super max institutions: the correctional facilities that feature the highest level of security. The inmates of a super max institution are housed individually and spend all but one hour of every day in their cell. On the rare occasions that inmates are allowed out of their cells, they are typically strip searched, guarded by multiple officers, and placed in full restraints. Most programs, however, are conducted via correspondence or closed-circuit television without the prisoner leaving the cell.

Other programs, in particular religious services, are conducted through the cell door.

Three piece suit: the informal name given to the full set of restraints (handcuffs, leg irons, and waist or belly chain)

Training: any activity that aims to teach the prisoners skills that will improve their job performance. Training may be conducted in person, and may be at a specialized training facility.

Type I facility: a minimum security correctional facility; this type of correctional facility is typically designed to help reintegrate into society those prisoners who are near the end of their term

Type II facility: a type of low security correctional facility in which the primary objective is to meet the labor needs of the institution; the inmates in a Type II facility typically have less than a year and a half (18 months) until their release date

Unit Management: the basic system through which a group of officers or counselors manage a wing or cell block of a prison. In order for the principles of unit management to be applicable, the unit must hold no more than 500 inmates, and ideally will hold less than 150. Also, there must be little turnover within the unit in order for the system to be effective. The officers and counselors assigned to the unit will work with the same unit for a long period of time, and will be given most of the decision-making responsibilities regarding programming and living conditions. All general conditions and regulations will be decided by the facility managers. Unit management is designed to increase contact between staff and inmates, so that strong working relationships can be built.

Unity of command: the principle of organizational hierarchy which asserts that it is most effective when a worker only has to report to one boss

Universal precautions: the essential practices of safety and medical care that aim to reduce the spread of disease

Urine surveillance program: the random but frequent collection of urine samples to check for drug use

Volunteer: any person who donates time to improving the programs and activities in a correctional facility

Warden: the chief executive or administrative officer of a correctional facility; also known as the superintendent

Work release: a system whereby inmates are released from a correctional facility in order to work at a place of business sanctioned by the government

Civil rights law suits

There are two basic kinds of civil rights claim regularly brought against correctional institutions. In the first, the plaintiff alleges that the policies or procedures of the institution infringe upon his or her rights. In the second, the plaintiff alleges that an officer of the correctional facility failed to act in accordance with the policies and procedures of the institution, and thereby infringed upon the plaintiff's civil rights. For a correctional officer, the best defense against the latter suit is to learn and abide by the policies of the institution. The first kind of claim will only affect the career of an individual officer insofar as it affects the function of the institution as a whole.

Courts play in the judicial system

As regards the correctional system, the courts seek to protect the rights of prisoners while making sure that officers of the law are protected. One of the major issues addressed by the court system is what constitutes "cruel and unusual punishment." In some cases, the court system is unable to achieve a clear ruling, and so correctional institutions are left to interpret the law as they see fit.

The Supreme Court

There are three eras of the Supreme Court's relationship with corrections in the United States: Hands-Off, Hands-On, and One Hand On, One Hand Off.

Until the 1960s, the Supreme Court took a hands-off approach, rejecting prisoner lawsuits regarding conditions of confinement. The justification for this approach was that corrections officials knew more about running prisons than did judges. Moreover, society showed little concern for prison conditions.

During the 1960s and 1970s, the Supreme Court focused on civil rights, deciding landmark desegregation (Brown v. Board of Education) and suspect rights cases (Miranda v. Arizona). The court began to take a hands-on approach to prison conditions, leading to recognition that even inmates have some constitutional rights.

More recently, the court has taken a One Hand Off, One Hand On approach. The court recognizes that the constitution guarantees certain minimum standards for prison conditions. Out of deference to prison officials, however, the court has placed the burden on inmates to prove violations.

The Prison Litigation Reform Act

The Prison Litigation Reform Act, passed in the 1990s, aimed to stem the flood of lawsuits in which inmates claimed violations of their civil rights. This act made it more difficult for prisoners to file frivolous suits, basically by forcing them to pay for their own legal fees. Also, any prisoner who had three suits dismissed was banned from filing any more without being in imminent danger and paying the entire filing fee up front. The act also encourages prisoners to try settling their complaints through administrative channels before entering the courts system.

Inmate litigation

There are three general categories of inmate litigation: tort suits, habeas corpus actions, and civil rights actions. A tort suit is filed in cases where an inmate claims to have been damaged or endangered because of the negligence of someone else. A habeas corpus action is filed when the inmate questions the constitutionality of his or her being in prison. This kind of case typically hinges on whether a certain kind of incarceration is determined to be cruel and unusual. Finally, a civil rights action is brought when an inmate asserts that his or her constitutional rights have been violated by the conditions or policies of the institution, or by the actions of an officer.

If it is determined that an inmate's rights have been violated, he or she may receive either an injunction or damages. An injunction is a court order that tells the agency or institution to stop a certain activity that has been deemed a violation of the prisoner's rights. This is the most common victory won by prisoners, and is the motivation for most of the changes in correctional policy. The PLRA asserts that the directions given by injunctions must be as specific and unobtrusive as possible. Prisoners may also win damages, which may be punitive, compensatory, or nominal. Punitive damages are large awards that are intended to prevent similar violations of a prisoner's constitutional rights in the future. Compensatory damages are in the form of wages lost or medical bills incurred because of the actions of the defendant. Nominal damages are small amounts awarded to the plaintiff mainly for symbolic purposes.

Agency and the supervisor liability

There are three common situations in which an agency and/or supervisor can be deemed liable for a correction officer's violation of an inmate's civil rights. The first is if there is a failure to supervise, meaning that the supervisor can be proven to have known about a violation of civil rights but to have remained "deliberately indifferent." If a supervisor tacitly condones a violation of the prisoner's rights, he or she can be held accountable. Another situation in which the supervisor or agency may be charged is in a case of failure to train, when the officer is required to perform duties for which he or she should have been trained but has not been. Finally, a supervisor or agency may be held accountable in situations where there is improper supervision, where there have been gross failures in hiring and firing, and when there is ineffective leadership.

In most cases, a state employee who is sued for a tort claim will be defended by the attorney general, and will have his or her costs of litigation indemnified. The scenarios in which the state will defend an employee vary by jurisdiction. As a general rule, however, states are more willing to defend employees for a minor infraction than for a serious criminal infraction.

"Access to courts"

Correctional facilities are required by law to give prisoners some access to legal materials. Because so many inmates are illiterate, institutions must not only provide law books but must offer legal education programs and reading classes. Inmates are also informed about the PLRA, which discourages them from filing frivolous lawsuits.

The different types of "discovery."

In a court setting, discovery is the right of each side to obtain all useful information before the case is tried. There are a few different ways by which this information may be gathered. A deposition is when a lawyer from one side of the case interviews a witness from the other side in the presence of a court reporter. The counsel on one side may also submit a written questionnaire, known as an interrogatory, which the recipient is required to complete under oath. Finally, a person on the other side of the case may be given a chance to admit or deny a statement. If the person does not deny or object to the statement within a certain amount of time, the statement will be admitted into evidence.

Some trial avoidance techniques

There are a few different ways to avoid going to trial. Many trials are avoided though out of court settlements, while others are dismissed before they go to trial. The defendant may file a Motion to Dismiss, otherwise known as a Rule 12 (b)(6) motion, which declares that even if all of the allegations made by the plaintiff are true, the plaintiff's rights have not been violated. Another document that can eliminate the need for a trial is a Summary Judgment, in which both sides agree to the material facts of the case and ask a judge to rule on these facts without trial.

List some good rules for testifying witnesses to follow

When testifying in court, witnesses should dress well, arrive early, and speak clearly. Witnesses should be familiar with their testimony, but should not memorize responses. Witnesses should always answer "yes" or "no" without volunteering extra information. If an incorrect answer is given by mistake, a witness should correct it immediately. Witnesses should never exaggerate, and should not be afraid to plead ignorance. A witness should always be courteous to both attorneys. If the witness is either the plaintiff or defendant, he or she should give his or her attorney time to object after each question. Witnesses should always stop talking when the judge interrupts, and, most importantly, should always tell the truth according to the best of their abilities.

Practice Test

Practice Questions

1. Which of the following is most important for preventing riots or other disturbances?
   a. Regularly practicing a well-planned crisis intervention plan
   b. Regular group talks given to inmates by the warden or other authority figures
   c. Consistent enforcement of rules and regulations
   d. Fast and detailed reporting of inmate infractions

2. Are inmates allowed to smoke?
   a. Yes
   b. No
   c. They may smoke in their cells, but not in common areas.
   d. The answer varies by jurisdiction.

3. True or False: It is important for correction officers to become friendly with inmates because it promotes understanding and mutual respect.
   True
   False

4. Which of the following is NOT a valid method of rewarding or punishing inmates?
   a. Solitary confinement
   b. Time off for good behavior
   c. Loss of inmate privileges
   d. Blocking mail from an inmate's attorney

5. While making rounds, you recognize a new inmate as a friend from high school you later lost contact with. You have not seen him in nearly 10 years. What should you do?
   a. Nothing, as this sort of thing happens from time to time
   b. Notify your supervisor
   c. Acknowledge the inmate in some way
   d. Offer to show him how to stay out of trouble

6. What is the most important component of a fire safety plan?
   a. Prevention
   b. Fire drills
   c. Learning how to use fire extinguishers
   d. Knowing where each fire extinguisher is located

7. What should you do in the case of a prisoner who is unconscious and might be having a heart attack?
    a. Call for medical assistance and begin mouth-to-mouth resuscitation
    b. Call for medical assistance, skip mouth-to-mouth resuscitation and give chest compressions at a rate of 50 per minute
    c. Call for medical assistance, skip mouth-to-mouth resuscitation and give chest compressions at a rate of 100 per minute
    d. Inform your supervisor and do nothing until medical assistance arrives

8. A police officer who arrests a person is required to "read him his rights," such as the right to remain silent and the right to an attorney. These rights are commonly referred to as…
    a. Civil rights.
    b. Arrest rights.
    c. Three strike rights.
    d. Miranda rights.

9. An inmate is entitled to have his rights read to him in which of the following situations?
    a. When he is separated from other inmates and questioned about criminal activity.
    b. When an undercover officer is put in his cell posing as a fellow inmate.
    c. Every time his cell is searched for contraband, even if his cellmate is the suspect.
    d. Every morning at first head count.

10. What is the main function of disciplinary actions against inmates?
    a. Teaching the inmate a lesson
    b. Maintaining order in the institution
    c. Establishing a degree of vengeance
    d. Rehabilitation of the inmate

11. Dealing with inmates with which of these conditions would NOT require extra precautions to protect the health of officers and fellow inmates?
    a. Hepatitis C
    b. AIDS
    c. Cancer
    d. Avian flu

12. True or False: An officer may legally refuse to touch a homosexual inmate if he has religious convictions against homosexuality.
    True
    False

13. What is the purpose of a shadow board?
    a. To keep track of officer assignments
    b. To make preventing escape attempts easier
    c. To make noticing missing tools easier
    d. To keep track of the progress of union grievances

14. What is the limit on how many times a month an inmate is allowed to meet with his attorney?
    a. A maximum of five times
    b. A maximum of 10 times
    c. A maximum of once a month
    d. There is no maximum

15. How often should keys, tools and other equipment be inventoried?
    a. Once a week
    b. Once a day
    c. At every shift change
    d. Every two hours

16. When moving a group of inmates, an officer should walk...
    a. Behind the group.
    b. Ahead of the group.
    c. To the side of the group.
    d. In the middle of the group.

17. Which of the following is a sign that trouble might be imminent?
    a. An inmate doesn't eat lunch, saying he's not hungry.
    b. An inmate seems to have gained weight in a day.
    c. An inmate says he's sick and asks to see a doctor.
    d. An inmate requests a different cell mate.

18. You and another officer are overseeing a large number of inmates in the recreation room. Suddenly a loud and angry argument breaks out between some small groups, and then two inmates begin shoving each other. What should you do?
    a. Call for backup
    b. Make a mental note to file a report later
    c. You and the other officer should move in to stop the fighting
    d. Call your supervisor and ask for advice

19. You observe another officer giving an inmate a small object in exchange for money. Neither one is aware that you have seen them. What should you do?
    a. Walk over and ask them what is going on
    b. Report the incident to your supervisor
    c. Request a different assignment in the future
    d. Nothing, because it is probably irrelevant

20. True or False: It is appropriate to fire a warning shot if a group of inmates is attacking an individual inmate.
    True
    False

21. Which of the following could be used as a weapon?
    a. Fork
    b. Knife
    c. Spoon
    d. All of the above

22. Many people believe that punishing criminals harshly reduces crime because the fear of going to jail or prison keeps many people from committing crimes. Which word best describes this effect?
    a. Rehabilitation
    b. Deterrence
    c. Incarceration
    d. Recidivism

23. Which of the following is NOT one of the main purposes of incarcerating criminals?
    a. To show other people that crime does not pay.
    b. To protect the public from criminals.
    c. To teach criminals a better way of life.
    d. To help criminals earn a college degree.

24. Which of the following would constitute reasonable grounds for searching an inmate?
    a. The inmate is serving a sentence for drug smuggling.
    b. The inmate makes rude or obnoxious remarks to an officer.
    c. The inmate appears nervous and is walking oddly.
    d. The inmate is not working hard on his job assignment.

25. True or False: An inmate convicted of sexual crimes against children cannot be forced to attend treatment programs for pedophiles while his case is on appeal.
    True
    False

26. A jail inmate who is currently on trial for murder begs his attorney to allow him to take a polygraph test. His attorney makes the arrangements, and the inmate fails the test miserably. How will this affect his trial?
    a. It will not affect it at all.
    b. The judge will tell the jury to consider the polygraph results.
    c. The judge will end the trial and declare the inmate guilty.
    d. The judge will ask the prosecutor how he or she wants to proceed.

27. At shift change, a key is missing. You should report this to your supervisor…
    a. At next shift change.
    b. At once.
    c. During your next break.
    d. After you have spent at least 30 minutes looking for it.

28. Why was the Prison Litigation Reform Act passed?
    a. To provide inmates with attorneys to file lawsuits against correctional facilities.
    b. To provide funds to train inmates to file their own lawsuits.
    c. To reduce the number of lawsuits filed by inmates.
    d. To create a special court reserved for inmate lawsuits.

29. Which of the following would be unethical behavior for a correction officer?
    a. Reporting late for work due to oversleeping.
    b. Working as much overtime as possible.
    c. Filing a grievance against a supervisor.
    d. Signing off on an incident report that contains inaccuracies.

30. Which of the following is NOT a common complaint of lawsuits against jails and prisons?
    a. The facilities are much too crowded.
    b. The health care is inadequate and a threat to inmates' health.
    c. Each day begins with a prayer over the intercom.
    d. The food served is lacking in quality and nutrition.

31. Which of the following is NOT one of the three most common complaints from families of people who committed suicide while incarcerated?
    a. The institution failed to identify the inmate as a suicide risk.
    b. The institution failed to notify the family of the suicide on a timely basis.
    c. The institution failed to monitor the inmate to prevent the suicide.
    d. The institution failed to respond in time when doing so could have saved the inmate.

32. In most situations it is best for a correction officer to…
    a. Follow official policies and procedures as closely as possible.
    b. Use his best judgment about what to do in each situation.
    c. Consult with fellow officers about what to do when that is an option.
    d. Use his discretion while being guided by official policies and procedures.

33. The most dangerous period for inmate suicide attempts is…
    a. The first week of incarceration.
    b. The first hour of incarceration.
    c. The first 24 hours of incarceration.
    d. The first month of incarceration.

34. True or False: Because of non-discrimination laws, a female inmate has no right to request a female correction officer for a strip search.
    True
    False

35. Which kind of correctional institution is often accused of refusing early release to inmates in order to make more money?
    a. Local jails
    b. Private prisons
    c. State prisons
    d. Federal prisons

36. True or False: Minorities are a higher percentage of the inmate population than of the overall population.
    True
    False

37. There are more men in prisons and jails than there are women. What is the ratio of incarcerated men to incarcerated women?
    a. 23 to 1
    b. 9 to 1
    c. 4 to 1
    d. 15 to 1

38. True or False: Jails and prisons are required by law to have a workforce whose racial demographics match those of the institution's inmate population.
    True
    False

39. Which of the following is NOT a requirement for a successful career as a correction officer?
    a. A commitment to honesty
    b. A commitment to integrity
    c. A commitment to continuous improvement
    d. A commitment to non-violence

40. What is the best schedule for searching cells for contraband?
    a. Once a week at the same day and time
    b. Once a month at the same day and time
    c. Once a month on the same day, but at different times
    d. There should be no set schedule

41. Does a correction officer have to join a union?
    a. It depends on the state in which the officer works.
    b. Yes; every correction officer is required to join a union.
    c. No; no correction officer is required to join a union.
    d. An officer must join a union if he wants to be eligible for early retirement.

42. Under what conditions may a correction officer keep a personal weapon in his or her car while parked in the employee parking lot?
    a. A correction officer should never keep a personal weapon in his or her car in the parking lot.
    b. If he or she has a concealed carry permit.
    c. If he or she has a concealed carry permit and written permission from her supervisor.
    d. If he or she has a concealed carry permit and keeps the weapon in the trunk, unloaded.

43. What happens to the personal property of inmates (watches, wallets, clothes) that is removed from them at intake?
    a. It is cataloged, stored and given back when they are released.
    b. It is auctioned off online and the proceeds are used toward paying court costs.
    c. It is stored until all appeals are exhausted; they get it back if they win their appeal, it is sold to pay court costs if they lose their appeal.
    d. It is given back to them once they are assigned a cell.

44. Which of the following would be considered a medical emergency?
    a. An inmate has the flu.
    b. An inmate has chest pain and numbness in his arm.
    c. An inmate has been hiccupping for three hours straight.
    d. An inmate has vomited.

45. If an inmate escapes, which items below should be included in the information provided to the public to in order to assist them to be on the lookout for him?
    a. Age
    b. Height
    c. Race
    d. All of the above

46. Approximately what percentage of federal prison inmates are in the United States illegally?
    a. Five percent
    b. 30 percent
    c. 15 percent
    d. 10 percent

47. True or False: There are times when a correction officer must devise and impose discipline on an inmate on the spot when they have committed an infraction.
    True
    False

48. Which of the following would constitute sexual harassment?
    a. A supervisor offers to give an officer a good review in exchange for sexual favors.
    b. A female officer continues to tell "dirty jokes" even after a male officer objects.
    c. An officer mounts a picture of a nude centerfold model in the break room.
    d. All of the above.

49. Which of the following is the biggest health hazard for correction officers?
    a. Assaults by inmates
    b. Injuries during riots
    c. Job-related stress
    d. Acquiring AIDS from an inmate

50. Which of the following methods of dealing with job stress should be a last resort?
    a. Prescription drugs
    b. Meditation
    c. Deep breathing
    d. Visualization techniques

Answers and Explanations

1. **C:** There are many factors that go into maintaining a calm and safe environment in a correctional institution, and one of the most important is that rules and regulations must be consistently enforced. Laxity, favoritism and other forms of inconsistency can lead to anger and resentment and should be avoided at all costs.

2. **D:** Rules about cigarette smoking and other tobacco use vary by jurisdiction. Until not long ago, virtually all jails and prisons in the United States allowed inmates (and staff) to smoke. Concerns about rising health care costs for both smokers and non-smokers led many states to ban smoking in correctional institutions, starting a few decades ago. More than half of the 50 states currently ban smoking, and that number is expected to keep rising.

3. **False:** Staff members must NOT become friendly with inmates (or members of their families), but should always strive to maintain a professional distance between themselves and inmates. This is not to suggest that correction workers should not care about the welfare of inmates; they should. However, they should not become friendly with them because doing so can cause substantial conflicts of interest.

4. **D:** Inmates have a right to communicate with their attorneys, and correctional institutions may not block mail to or from an inmate's lawyer. Doing so would be an unconstitutional form of punishment. The other choices are all valid methods for rewarding or punishing inmates.

5. **B:** If you come across an inmate you know while working in corrections, you should immediately inform your direct supervisor. This includes close relatives, distant relatives, current friends, friends you have not seen for years, friends you have had a falling out with, former co-workers, and all other past and present acquaintances. The potential for a conflict of interest is high in a situation like this, and failing to notify your supervisor immediately could lead to disciplinary action.

6. **A:** Fire prevention is the most important aspect of a fire safety program. This is not to downplay the importance of knowing where the fire extinguishers are and how to use them, or the necessity of holding regular fire drills. These are all important. However, the best way of keeping people and property safe from fires is making sure one never starts.

7. **A:** You should request medical assistance and immediately begin mouth-to-mouth resuscitation. This is the general rule, but there could be times when you might have to ignore the rule if following it might endanger you, another officer, or other inmates.

8. D: Miranda rights are named after a lawsuit, *Miranda vs. Arizona*. Here is the Miranda warning given to arrestees: "You have the right to remain silent. Anything you say or do may be used against you in a court of law. You have the right to consult an attorney before speaking to the police and to have an attorney present during questioning now or in the future. If you cannot afford an attorney, one will be appointed for you before any questioning, if you wish. If you decide to answer any questions now, without an attorney present, you will still have the right to stop answering at any time until you talk to an attorney. Knowing and understanding your rights as I have explained them to you, are you willing to answer my questions without an attorney present?"

9. A: You are not required to read an inmate his rights when you are carrying out the day-to-day activities of a correctional institution, such as head count or cell searches for contraband. Undercover officers posing as inmates are also not required to reveal what they are doing. But if an inmate is separated from the rest of the inmate population and questioned about criminal activity, this is considered an interrogation, and that inmate is entitled to a reading of his rights before it begins.

10. B: The main function of disciplinary action is to maintain order in the institution. It should never be used to exact vengeance or "teach someone a lesson." Also, while disciplinary action is not primarily designed to rehabilitate inmates, such rehabilitation may occur in some inmates as a result of maintaining order.

11. C: Cancer is neither infectious nor contagious. All of the other health conditions listed can possibly be spread to others, so proper precautions must be taken to protect the health of officers and other inmates. Your institution will have detailed policies and procedure for handling such situations.

12. False: There is no such right recognized by a court of law anywhere in the United States. Inmates are entitled to equal treatment no matter their sexual orientation or the religious beliefs of officers or other correction personnel.

13. C: Tools can be used as weapons against officers or other inmates, and can be used to help facilitate an escape attempt. For this reason they are kept on wall boards with an outline of each tool drawn around its storage position. This makes it instantly obvious when a tool goes missing.

14. D: The right to counsel is a fundamental constitutional right, and correctional institutions may not infringe upon it. This does not mean that an inmate can force a jail or prison to allow him to meet with his attorney at 3:00 in the morning, or meet with him every day for hours on end on a regular basis. However, there may be times when an inmate needs to spend a lot of time with his attorney, and institutions cannot have arbitrary policies that interfere, such as a maximum number of meetings per month.

15. C: Each officer is responsible for his keys, tools and equipment issued to him during his shift. In order to keep track of them, they must be accounted for at the beginning and end of every shift. If something is missing, the supervisor must be notified at once. An officer should never falsely sign off on a short count.

16. A: Walking behind a group of inmates is necessary for the safety of the officer, as it prevents surprise attacks. Any officer walking to the side would have limited sight of the entire group, and an officer in front would have zero sight.

17. B: All of the other choices represent what are usually normal everyday events with perfectly reasonable explanations. An inmate may not be getting along with his cell mate, or he may actually be sick, or he may not feel hungry. None of these are cause for concern in and of themselves. But sudden changes in physical appearance, such as noticeable weight gain in a few hours or days, is often a sign that something is very wrong.

18. A: A situation such as this is extremely dangerous, and two officers are not sufficient to get the situation back under control by themselves. There is no time to call for advice; you must get officers in the room immediately before things get even further out of hand, both for your own safety and the safety of the inmates.

19. B: You are a correction officer, not a police officer or a prosecutor, so it is not your place to confront the officer and the inmate; doing so could cause a very bad situation. It is also not your place to ignore the incident and do nothing or to ask for a different assignment. You should report the incident to your immediate supervisor as soon as practically possible.

20. False: Firing a gun is using lethal force, and should only be used in cases where someone is using deadly force against another person, or seems about to, such as when an inmate possesses a gun and threatens to shoot someone with it. Also, you should never use your gun to fire a "warning shot."

21. D: All of the above could be, and have been, used as weapons by inmates and criminals. A spoon used as a weapon can be dangerous, despite how harmless it may seem. A person could be maimed for life or even killed after being attacked with a spoon.

22. B: Rehabilitation is the process of helping inmates turn away from crime and make better choices. Incarceration is just another name for imprisonment. Recidivism refers to a person going back to jail or prison after being released because they return to a life of crime.

23. D: Deterrence is one of the aims of incarceration—when people see others going to prison for a long time, they tend to reconsider committing a crime themselves. Keeping the public safe from criminals is also one of the goals. The third main goal is

helping criminals see the error of their ways and learn to live better; this is called rehabilitation. Allowing inmates to earn a college degree can be part of the rehabilitation process, but it is not one of the main goals of incarceration.

24. C: A correction officer must have a valid reason to search an inmate. In other words, there must be something that causes the officer to believe that the inmate is hiding something on his person. An inmate who is nervous and walking oddly certainly falls into this category, as it is likely that he is walking oddly because he is trying to conceal something, and his being nervous is a good sign that he is worried about being caught.

25. True: Treatment programs for pedophiles require the clients to admit that they are sexually attracted to children. Forcing an inmate to attend one while his case is still under appeal is seen as a violation of his rights. Only after his appeals have been exhausted can he be forced to attend.

26. A: It will not change the trial at all. Polygraph results are not admissible in courts, even if the defendant volunteers to take one. His attorney would have no obligation to share the results with the judge, prosecutor, or jury.

27. B: A missing key could allow an inmate or several inmates into an unauthorized area. It must be reported at once.

28. C: Many inmates believe they have received unfair treatment somewhere during the process of their incarceration—they did not get a fair trial, the prison is violating their rights, or some other injustice has befallen them. Others are simply bored and turn to researching and filing lawsuits as a hobby. At any rate, the number of lawsuits by inmates was clogging the courts, and the act was passed in order to address this problem.

29. D. Oversleeping and being late for work should be avoided as much as possible, but it can happen. As long as it was not deliberate or due to gross negligence (staying out all night partying) and the officer does not lie about it, it is not unethical. There is also nothing unethical about working lots of overtime or filing legitimate grievances. But an officer signing a report that he or she knows is not entirely truthful is highly unethical.

30. C: Overcrowding, lack of access to adequate health care, and food of low quality and nutritional value are all common complaints of inmate lawsuits, as well as lawsuits brought by others on behalf of inmates. However, these are far from the only reasons people file lawsuits against correctional institutions.

31. B: While it is not unheard of for relatives to complain that there was a delay in notifying them of an inmate suicide, it is not one of the most common complaints around this subject. The three most common are the other ones listed.

32. A: A correction officer should always follow official policies and procedures to the best of his abilities, at all times, and in every situation. There are very few situations a correction officer will ever encounter that are not covered by official policies and procedures.

33. C: A very high percentage of suicide attempts take place within an inmate's first 24 hours of incarceration. There are a variety of reasons for this—drug and alcohol withdrawal, shock at being incarcerated, and depression over bad life choices, to name a few. This is not to imply that this is the only period when inmates attempt suicide, but only that correction officers should be more vigilant about monitoring the inmate during this period.

34. False: Only female correction officers may conduct a strip search of female inmates. However, according to current court rulings, both male and female officers are allowed to conduct strip searches of male inmates.

35. B: Private prisons are run by corporations in order to make a profit. They charge the government a certain amount of money per day, per inmate. This naturally leads many people to suspect that one of the main reasons private prisons deny an inmate early release is to maintain profits for as long as possible.

36. True: African-Americans are about 14 percent of the American male population, but about 40 percent of the prison population. Hispanics are also overrepresented. In 2010, 43 out of every 1,000 black males were in jail or prison. For Hispanic males, the number was 18 out of every 1,000. For white males, the number was seven for every 1000.

37. B: There are about nine times as many men in jails and prisons as there are women. This ratio is fairly consistent all over the country, and has held steady for many decades.

38. False: There is no law making that a requirement and, if such a law existed, it would probably be ruled unconstitutional.

39. D: A commitment to non-violence is not an acceptable trait in a correction officer. Of course, an officer should avoid engaging in violent behavior as much as possible, and that sometimes means taking a lot of verbal abuse from inmates. But there will be times in most officers' careers that using violence to restrain an inmate or inmates is necessary, so a man with a philosophical commitment to non-violence would have to choose between violating his beliefs or endangering himself and others.

40. D: Routine searches conducted on a regularly scheduled basis remove one of the most important elements of a cell search, which is surprise. Routine searches should be conducted on a randomized basis.

41. A: In some states, correction officers are required to join and pay union dues to the labor union authorized to represent officers. In other states, called "right to work" states, union membership is not required.

42. A: Because of safety concerns, correction officers are not allowed to keep a personal weapon in their car while parked on the grounds of the correctional institution, even if they possess a lawful permit to carry a concealed weapon. This is to eliminate the risk that an escapee or someone else could break into the vehicle and take the weapon.

43. A: Personal property is taken from inmates upon intake and recorded and stored until their release, at which time it is given back to them. In many institutions an inmate may authorize the institution to release their property to a person they choose. If they don't make this choice, their property is held until their release.

44. B: Chest pain and numbness in the arm are two symptoms which could indicate a heart attack and the inmate should get medical help immediately. In the other situations, there is a good chance that the inmate will need to see a doctor in the very near future, but none of them would constitute an emergency situation in and of themselves.

45. D: The public should be given as much information as possible to help them identify an escaped convict, such as gender, race, height, weight, age, scars, tattoos, and any other identifying features. The more information the public has, the more likely it is that someone will be able to identify the escapee.

46. B: Official figures vary somewhat, but most experts say that between 27 and 33 percent of federal prison inmates are in the United States illegally.

47. False: A correction officer has no authority to punish or discipline inmates for any infractions, whether serious or minor. The officer must report the infraction to a supervisor and let the proper authorities decide on a punishment.

48. D: All of the scenarios would be considered sexual harassment. Sexual harassment is much broader than someone making an offer of better treatment in exchange for sexual favors, and includes any unwelcome behavior of a sexual nature. It is best to avoid any hint of sexual behavior or conversation at work.

49. C: The chances of acquiring AIDS from an inmate are very low, as are the chances of being injured during a riot. Being assaulted by an inmate is more likely than these two, but even that does not result in stress when it comes to overall damage to an officer's long-term health. Health experts say that stress that is not dealt with can take years off of a person's life expectancy.

50. A: Generally speaking, it is best to avoid taking drugs unless absolutely necessary. Side effects can be very bad, and the drugs might lead to a lower level of job performance, even if only taken after a shift. Natural remedies should be attempted first. Of course, if your physician prescribes a drug, you should follow his advice, but if there is any chance the drug could affect your work, you should let your supervisor know about the situation.

Secret Key #1 - Time is Your Greatest Enemy

Pace Yourself

Wear a watch. At the beginning of the test, check the time (or start a chronometer on your watch to count the minutes), and check the time after every few questions to make sure you are "on schedule."

If you are forced to speed up, do it efficiently. Usually one or more answer choices can be eliminated without too much difficulty. Above all, don't panic. Don't speed up and just begin guessing at random choices. By pacing yourself, and continually monitoring your progress against your watch, you will always know exactly how far ahead or behind you are with your available time. If you find that you are one minute behind on the test, don't skip one question without spending any time on it, just to catch back up. Take 15 fewer seconds on the next four questions, and after four questions you'll have caught back up. Once you catch back up, you can continue working each problem at your normal pace.

Furthermore, don't dwell on the problems that you were rushed on. If a problem was taking up too much time and you made a hurried guess, it must be difficult. The difficult questions are the ones you are most likely to miss anyway, so it isn't a big loss. It is better to end with more time than you need than to run out of time.

Lastly, sometimes it is beneficial to slow down if you are constantly getting ahead of time. You are always more likely to catch a careless mistake by working more slowly than quickly, and among very high-scoring test takers (those who are likely to have lots of time left over), careless errors affect the score more than mastery of material.

Secret Key #2 - Guessing is not Guesswork

You probably know that guessing is a good idea - unlike other standardized tests, there is no penalty for getting a wrong answer. Even if you have no idea about a question, you still have a 20-25% chance of getting it right.

Most test takers do not understand the impact that proper guessing can have on their score. Unless you score extremely high, guessing will significantly contribute to your final score.

Monkeys Take the Test

What most test takers don't realize is that to insure that 20-25% chance, you have to guess randomly. If you put 20 monkeys in a room to take this test, assuming they answered once per question and behaved themselves, on average they would get 20-25% of the questions correct. Put 20 test takers in the room, and the average will be much lower among guessed questions. Why?

1. The test writers intentionally writes deceptive answer choices that "look" right. A test taker has no idea about a question, so picks the "best looking" answer, which is often wrong. The monkey has no idea what looks good and what doesn't, so will consistently be lucky about 20-25% of the time.

2. Test takers will eliminate answer choices from the guessing pool based on a hunch or intuition. Simple but correct answers often get excluded, leaving a 0% chance of being correct. The monkey has no clue, and often gets lucky with the best choice.

This is why the process of elimination endorsed by most test courses is flawed and detrimental to your performance- test takers don't guess, they make an ignorant stab in the dark that is usually worse than random.

$5 Challenge

Let me introduce one of the most valuable ideas of this course- the $5 challenge:

You only mark your "best guess" if you are willing to bet $5 on it.

You only eliminate choices from guessing if you are willing to bet $5 on it.

Why $5? Five dollars is an amount of money that is small yet not insignificant, and can really add up fast (20 questions could cost you $100). Likewise, each answer choice on one question of the test will have a small impact on your overall score, but it can really add up to a lot of points in the end.

The process of elimination IS valuable. The following shows your chance of guessing it right:

If you eliminate wrong answer choices until only this many remain:	1	2	3
Chance of getting it correct:	100%	50%	33%

However, if you accidentally eliminate the right answer or go on a hunch for an incorrect answer, your chances drop dramatically: to 0%. By guessing among all the answer choices, you are GUARANTEED to have a shot at the right answer.

That's why the $5 test is so valuable- if you give up the advantage and safety of a pure guess, it had better be worth the risk.

What we still haven't covered is how to be sure that whatever guess you make is truly random. Here's the easiest way:

Always pick the first answer choice among those remaining.

Such a technique means that you have decided, **before you see a single test question**, exactly how you are going to guess- and since the order of choices tells you nothing about which one is correct, this guessing technique is perfectly random.

This section is not meant to scare you away from making educated guesses or eliminating choices- you just need to define when a choice is worth eliminating. The $5 test, along with a pre-defined random guessing strategy, is the best way to make sure you reap all of the benefits of guessing.

Secret Key #3 - Practice Smarter, Not Harder

Many test takers delay the test preparation process because they dread the awful amounts of practice time they think necessary to succeed on the test. We have refined an effective method that will take you only a fraction of the time.

There are a number of "obstacles" in your way to succeed. Among these are answering questions, finishing in time, and mastering test-taking strategies. All must be executed on the day of the test at peak performance, or your score will suffer. The test is a mental marathon that has a large impact on your future.

Just like a marathon runner, it is important to work your way up to the full challenge. So first you just worry about questions, and then time, and finally strategy:

Success Strategy

1. Find a good source for practice tests.
2. If you are willing to make a larger time investment, consider using more than one study guide- often the different approaches of multiple authors will help you "get" difficult concepts.
3. Take a practice test with no time constraints, with all study helps "open book." Take your time with questions and focus on applying strategies.
4. Take a practice test with time constraints, with all guides "open book."
5. Take a final practice test with no open material and time limits

If you have time to take more practice tests, just repeat step 5. By gradually exposing yourself to the full rigors of the test environment, you will condition your mind to the stress of test day and maximize your success.

Secret Key #4 - Prepare, Don't Procrastinate

Let me state an obvious fact: if you take the test three times, you will get three different scores. This is due to the way you feel on test day, the level of preparedness you have, and, despite the test writers' claims to the contrary, some tests WILL be easier for you than others.

Since your future depends so much on your score, you should maximize your chances of success. In order to maximize the likelihood of success, you've got to prepare in advance. This means taking practice tests and spending time learning the information and test taking strategies you will need to succeed.

Never take the test as a "practice" test, expecting that you can just take it again if you need to. Feel free to take sample tests on your own, but when you go to take the official test, be prepared, be focused, and do your best the first time!

Secret Key #5 - Test Yourself

Everyone knows that time is money. There is no need to spend too much of your time or too little of your time preparing for the test. You should only spend as much of your precious time preparing as is necessary for you to get the score you need.

Once you have taken a practice test under real conditions of time constraints, then you will know if you are ready for the test or not.

If you have scored extremely high the first time that you take the practice test, then there is not much point in spending countless hours studying. You are already there.

Benchmark your abilities by retaking practice tests and seeing how much you have improved. Once you score high enough to guarantee success, then you are ready.

If you have scored well below where you need, then knuckle down and begin studying in earnest. Check your improvement regularly through the use of practice tests under real conditions. Above all, don't worry, panic, or give up. The key is perseverance!

Then, when you go to take the test, remain confident and remember how well you did on the practice tests. If you can score high enough on a practice test, then you can do the same on the real thing.

General Strategies

The most important thing you can do is to ignore your fears and jump into the test immediately- do not be overwhelmed by any strange-sounding terms. You have to jump into the test like jumping into a pool- all at once is the easiest way.

Make Predictions

As you read and understand the question, try to guess what the answer will be. Remember that several of the answer choices are wrong, and once you begin reading them, your mind will immediately become cluttered with answer choices designed to throw you off. Your mind is typically the most focused immediately after you have read the question and digested its contents. If you can, try to predict what the correct answer will be. You may be surprised at what you can predict.

Quickly scan the choices and see if your prediction is in the listed answer choices. If it is, then you can be quite confident that you have the right answer. It still won't hurt to check the other answer choices, but most of the time, you've got it!

Answer the Question

It may seem obvious to only pick answer choices that answer the question, but the test writers can create some excellent answer choices that are wrong. Don't pick an answer just because it sounds right, or you believe it to be true. It MUST answer the question. Once you've made your selection, always go back and check it against the question and make sure that you didn't misread the question, and the answer choice does answer the question posed.

Benchmark

After you read the first answer choice, decide if you think it sounds correct or not. If it doesn't, move on to the next answer choice. If it does, mentally mark that answer choice. This doesn't mean that you've definitely selected it as your answer choice, it just means that it's the best you've seen thus far. Go ahead and read the next choice. If the next choice is worse than the one you've already selected, keep going to the next answer choice. If the next choice is better than the choice you've already selected, mentally mark the new answer choice as your best guess.

The first answer choice that you select becomes your standard. Every other answer choice must be benchmarked against that standard. That choice is correct until proven otherwise by another answer choice beating it out. Once you've decided that no other answer choice seems as good, do one final check to ensure that your answer choice answers the question posed.

Valid Information

Don't discount any of the information provided in the question. Every piece of information may be necessary to determine the correct answer. None of the information in the question is there to throw you off (while the answer choices will certainly have information to throw you off). If two seemingly unrelated topics are discussed, don't ignore either. You can be confident there is a relationship, or it wouldn't be included in the question, and you are probably going to have to determine what is that relationship to find the answer.

Avoid "Fact Traps"

Don't get distracted by a choice that is factually true. Your search is for the answer that answers the question. Stay focused and don't fall for an answer that is true but incorrect. Always go back to the question and make sure you're choosing an answer that actually answers the question and is not just a true statement. An answer can be factually correct, but it MUST answer the question asked. Additionally, two answers can both be seemingly correct, so be sure to read all of the answer choices, and make sure that you get the one that BEST answers the question.

Milk the Question

Some of the questions may throw you completely off. They might deal with a

- 109 -

subject you have not been exposed to, or one that you haven't reviewed in years. While your lack of knowledge about the subject will be a hindrance, the question itself can give you many clues that will help you find the correct answer. Read the question carefully and look for clues. Watch particularly for adjectives and nouns describing difficult terms or words that you don't recognize. Regardless of if you completely understand a word or not, replacing it with a synonym either provided or one you more familiar with may help you to understand what the questions are asking. Rather than wracking your mind about specific detailed information concerning a difficult term or word, try to use mental substitutes that are easier to understand.

The Trap of Familiarity

Don't just choose a word because you recognize it. On difficult questions, you may not recognize a number of words in the answer choices. The test writers don't put "make-believe" words on the test; so don't think that just because you only recognize all the words in one answer choice means that answer choice must be correct. If you only recognize words in one answer choice, then focus on that one. Is it correct? Try your best to determine if it is correct. If it is, that is great, but if it doesn't, eliminate it. Each word and answer choice you eliminate increases your chances of getting the question correct, even if you then have to guess among the unfamiliar choices.

Eliminate Answers

Eliminate choices as soon as you realize they are wrong. But be careful! Make sure you consider all of the possible answer choices. Just because one appears right, doesn't mean that the next one won't be even better! The test writers will usually put more than one good answer choice for every question, so read all of them. Don't worry if you are stuck between two that seem right. By getting down to just two remaining possible choices, your odds are now 50/50. Rather than wasting too much time, play the odds. You are guessing, but guessing wisely, because you've been able to knock out some of the answer choices that you know are wrong. If you are eliminating choices and realize that the last answer choice you are left with is also obviously wrong, don't panic. Start over and consider each choice again. There may easily be something that you missed the first time and will realize on the second pass.

Tough Questions

If you are stumped on a problem or it appears too hard or too difficult, don't waste time. Move on! Remember though, if you can quickly check for obviously incorrect answer choices, your chances of guessing correctly are greatly improved. Before you completely give up, at least try to knock out a couple of possible answers. Eliminate what you can and then guess at the remaining answer choices before moving on.

Brainstorm

If you get stuck on a difficult question, spend a few seconds quickly brainstorming. Run through the complete list of possible answer choices. Look at each choice and ask yourself, "Could this answer the question satisfactorily?" Go through each answer choice and consider it independently of the other. By systematically going through all possibilities, you may find something that you would otherwise overlook. Remember that when you get stuck, it's important to try to keep moving.

Read Carefully

Understand the problem. Read the question and answer choices carefully. Don't miss the question because you misread the terms. You have plenty of time to read each question thoroughly and make sure you understand what is being asked. Yet a happy medium must be attained, so don't waste too much time. You must read carefully, but efficiently.

Face Value

When in doubt, use common sense. Always accept the situation in the problem at face value. Don't read too much into it. These problems will not require you to make huge leaps of logic. The test writers aren't trying to throw you off with a cheap trick. If you have to go beyond creativity and make a leap of logic in order to have an answer choice answer the question, then you should look at the other answer choices. Don't overcomplicate the problem by creating theoretical relationships or explanations that will warp time or space. These are normal problems rooted in reality. It's just that the applicable relationship or explanation may not be readily apparent and you have to figure things out. Use your common sense to interpret anything that isn't clear.

Prefixes

If you're having trouble with a word in the question or answer choices, try dissecting it. Take advantage of every clue that the word might include. Prefixes and suffixes can be a huge help. Usually they allow you to determine a basic meaning. Pre- means before, post- means after, pro - is positive, de- is negative. From these prefixes and suffixes, you can get an idea of the general meaning of the word and try to put it into context. Beware though of any traps. Just because con is the opposite of pro, doesn't necessarily mean congress is the opposite of progress!

Hedge Phrases

Watch out for critical "hedge" phrases, such as likely, may, can, will often, sometimes, often, almost, mostly, usually, generally, rarely, sometimes. Question writers insert these hedge phrases to cover every possibility. Often an answer choice will be wrong simply because it leaves no room for exception. Avoid answer choices that have definitive words like "exactly," and "always".

Switchback Words

Stay alert for "switchbacks". These are the words and phrases frequently used to alert you to shifts in thought. The most common switchback word is "but". Others include although, however, nevertheless, on the other hand, even though, while, in spite of, despite, regardless of.

New Information

Correct answer choices will rarely have completely new information included. Answer choices typically are straightforward reflections of the material asked about and will directly relate to the question. If a new piece of information is included in an answer choice that doesn't even seem to relate to the topic being asked about, then that answer choice is likely incorrect. All of the information needed to answer the question is usually provided for you, and so you should not have to make guesses that are unsupported or choose answer choices that require unknown information that cannot be reasoned on its own.

Time Management

On technical questions, don't get lost on the technical terms. Don't spend too much time on any one question. If you don't know what a term means, then since you don't have a dictionary, odds are you aren't going to get much further. You should immediately recognize terms as whether or not you know them. If you don't, work with the other clues that you have, the other answer choices and terms provided, but don't waste too much time trying to figure out a difficult term.

Contextual Clues

Look for contextual clues. An answer can be right but not correct. The contextual clues will help you find the answer that is most right and is correct. Understand the context in which a phrase or statement is made. This will help you make important distinctions.

Don't Panic

Panicking will not answer any questions for you. Therefore, it isn't helpful. When you first see the question, if your mind goes blank, take a deep breath. Force yourself to mechanically go through the steps of solving the problem and using the strategies you've learned.

Pace Yourself

Don't get clock fever. It's easy to be overwhelmed when you're looking at a page full of questions, your mind is full of random thoughts and feeling confused, and the clock is ticking down faster than you would like. Calm down and maintain the pace that you have set for yourself. As long as you are on track by monitoring your pace, you are guaranteed to have enough time for yourself. When you get to the last few minutes of the test, it may seem like you won't have enough time left, but if you only have as many questions as you should have left at that point, then you're right on track!

Answer Selection

The best way to pick an answer choice is to eliminate all of those that are wrong, until only one is left and confirm that is the correct answer. Sometimes though, an answer choice may immediately look right. Be careful! Take a second to make sure that the other choices are not equally obvious. Don't make a hasty mistake. There are only two times that you should stop before checking other answers. First is when you are positive that the answer choice you have selected is correct. Second is when time is almost out and you have to make a quick guess!

Check Your Work

Since you will probably not know every term listed and the answer to every question, it is important that you get credit for the ones that you do know. Don't miss any questions through careless mistakes. If at all possible, try to take a second to look back over your answer selection and make sure you've selected the correct answer choice and haven't made a costly careless mistake (such as marking an answer choice that you didn't mean to mark). This quick double check should more than pay for itself in caught mistakes for the time it costs.

Beware of Directly Quoted Answers

Sometimes an answer choice will repeat word for word a portion of the question or reference section. However, beware of such exact duplication – it may be a trap! More than likely, the correct choice will paraphrase or summarize a point, rather than being exactly the same wording.

Slang

Scientific sounding answers are better than slang ones. An answer choice that begins "To compare the outcomes…" is much more likely to be correct than one that begins "Because some people insisted…"

Extreme Statements

Avoid wild answers that throw out highly controversial ideas that are proclaimed as established fact. An answer choice that states the "process should be used in certain situations, if…" is much more likely to be correct than one that states the "process should be discontinued completely."   The first is a calm rational statement and doesn't even make a definitive, uncompromising stance, using a hedge word "if" to provide wiggle room, whereas the second choice is a radical idea and far more extreme.

Answer Choice Families

When you have two or more answer choices that are direct opposites or parallels, one of them is usually the correct answer. For instance, if one answer choice states "x increases" and another answer choice states "x decreases" or "y increases," then those two or three answer choices are very similar in construction and fall into the same family of answer choices. A family of answer choices is when two or three answer choices are very similar in construction, and yet often have a directly opposite meaning.   Usually the correct answer choice will be in that family of answer choices. The "odd man out" or answer choice that doesn't seem to fit the parallel construction of the other answer choices is more likely to be incorrect.

Special Report: What is Test Anxiety and How to Overcome It?

The very nature of tests caters to some level of anxiety, nervousness or tension, just as we feel for any important event that occurs in our lives. A little bit of anxiety or nervousness can be a good thing. It helps us with motivation, and makes achievement just that much sweeter. However, too much anxiety can be a problem; especially if it hinders our ability to function and perform.

"Test anxiety," is the term that refers to the emotional reactions that some test-takers experience when faced with a test or exam. Having a fear of testing and exams is based upon a rational fear, since the test-taker's performance can shape the course of an academic career. Nevertheless, experiencing excessive fear of examinations will only interfere with the test-takers ability to perform, and his/her chances to be successful.

There are a large variety of causes that can contribute to the development and sensation of test anxiety. These include, but are not limited to lack of performance and worrying about issues surrounding the test.

Lack of Preparation

Lack of preparation can be identified by the following behaviors or situations:

Not scheduling enough time to study, and therefore cramming the night before the test or exam
Managing time poorly, to create the sensation that there is not enough time to do everything

Failing to organize the text information in advance, so that the study material consists of the entire text and not simply the pertinent information

Poor overall studying habits

Worrying, on the other hand, can be related to both the test taker, or many other factors around him/her that will be affected by the results of the test. These include worrying about:

Previous performances on similar exams, or exams in general

How friends and other students are achieving

The negative consequences that will result from a poor grade or failure

There are three primary elements to test anxiety. Physical components, which involve the same typical bodily reactions as those to acute anxiety (to be discussed below). Emotional factors have to do with fear or panic. Mental or cognitive issues concerning attention spans and memory abilities.

Physical Signals

There are many different symptoms of test anxiety, and these are not limited to mental and emotional strain, Frequently there are a range of physical signals that will let a test taker know that he/she is suffering from test anxiety. These bodily changes can include the following:

Perspiring

Sweaty palms

Wet, trembling hands

Nausea

Dry mouth

A knot in the stomach

Headache

Faintness

Muscle tension

Aching shoulders, back and neck

Rapid heart beat

Feeling too hot/cold

To recognize the sensation of test anxiety, a test-taker should monitor
him/herself for the following sensations:

The physical distress symptoms as listed above

Emotional sensitivity, expressing emotional feelings such as the need to cry or
laugh too much, or a sensation of anger or helplessness

A decreased ability to think, causing the test-taker to blank out or have racing
thoughts that are hard to organize or control.

Though most students will feel some level of anxiety when faced with a test or
exam, the majority can cope with that anxiety and maintain it at a manageable
level. However, those who cannot are faced with a very real and very serious
condition, which can and should be controlled for the immeasurable benefit of
this sufferer.

Naturally, these sensations lead to negative results for the testing experience.
The most common effects of test anxiety have to do with nervousness and
mental blocking.

Nervousness

Nervousness can appear in several different levels:

The test-taker's difficulty, or even inability to read and understand the questions on the test

The difficulty or inability to organize thoughts to a coherent form

The difficulty or inability to recall key words and concepts relating to the testing questions (especially essays)

The receipt of poor grades on a test, though the test material was well known by the test taker

Conversely, a person may also experience mental blocking, which involves:

Blanking out on test questions

Only remembering the correct answers to the questions when the test has already finished.

Fortunately for test anxiety sufferers, beating these feelings, to a large degree, has to do with proper preparation. When a test taker has a feeling of preparedness, then anxiety will be dramatically lessened.

The first step to resolving anxiety issues is to distinguish which of the two types of anxiety are being suffered. If the anxiety is a direct result of a lack of preparation, this should be considered a normal reaction, and the anxiety level (as opposed to the test results) shouldn't be anything to worry about. However, if, when adequately prepared, the test-taker still panics, blanks out, or seems to overreact, this is not a fully rational reaction. While this can be considered normal too, there are many ways to combat and overcome these effects.

Remember that anxiety cannot be entirely eliminated, however, there are ways to minimize it, to make the anxiety easier to manage. Preparation is one of the best ways to minimize test anxiety. Therefore the following techniques are wise in order to best fight off any anxiety that may want to build.

To begin with, try to avoid cramming before a test, whenever it is possible. By trying to memorize an entire term's worth of information in one day, you'll be shocking your system, and not giving yourself a very good chance to absorb the information. This is an easy path to anxiety, so for those who suffer from test anxiety, cramming should not even be considered an option.

Instead of cramming, work throughout the semester to combine all of the material which is presented throughout the semester, and work on it gradually as the course goes by, making sure to master the main concepts first, leaving minor details for a week or so before the test.

To study for the upcoming exam, be sure to pose questions that may be on the examination, to gauge the ability to answer them by integrating the ideas from your texts, notes and lectures, as well as any supplementary readings.

If it is truly impossible to cover all of the information that was covered in that particular term, concentrate on the most important portions, that can be covered very well. Learn these concepts as best as possible, so that when the test comes, a goal can be made to use these concepts as presentations of your knowledge.

In addition to study habits, changes in attitude are critical to beating a struggle with test anxiety. In fact, an improvement of the perspective over the entire test-taking experience can actually help a test taker to enjoy studying and therefore improve the overall experience. Be certain not to overemphasize the significance of the grade - know that the result of the test is neither a reflection of self worth, nor is it a measure of intelligence; one grade will not predict a person's future success.

To improve an overall testing outlook, the following steps should be tried:

Keeping in mind that the most reasonable expectation for taking a test is to expect to try to demonstrate as much of what you know as you possibly can. Reminding ourselves that a test is only one test; this is not the only one, and there will be others.
The thought of thinking of oneself in an irrational, all-or-nothing term should be avoided at all costs.
A reward should be designated for after the test, so there's something to look forward to. Whether it be going to a movie, going out to eat, or simply visiting friends, schedule it in advance, and do it no matter what result is expected on the exam.

Test-takers should also keep in mind that the basics are some of the most important things, even beyond anti-anxiety techniques and studying. Never neglect the basic social, emotional and biological needs, in order to try to absorb information. In order to best achieve, these three factors must be held as just as important as the studying itself.

Study Steps

Remember the following important steps for studying:
Maintain healthy nutrition and exercise habits. Continue both your recreational activities and social pass times. These both contribute to your physical and emotional well being.

Be certain to get a good amount of sleep, especially the night before the test, because when you're overtired you are not able to perform to the best of your best ability.

Keep the studying pace to a moderate level by taking breaks when they are needed, and varying the work whenever possible, to keep the mind fresh instead of getting bored.

When enough studying has been done that all the material that can be learned has been learned, and the test taker is prepared for the test, stop studying and do something relaxing such as listening to music, watching a movie, or taking a warm bubble bath.

There are also many other techniques to minimize the uneasiness or apprehension that is experienced along with test anxiety before, during, or even after the examination. In fact, there are a great deal of things that can be done to stop anxiety from interfering with lifestyle and performance. Again, remember that anxiety will not be eliminated entirely, and it shouldn't be. Otherwise that "up" feeling for exams would not exist, and most of us depend on that sensation to perform better than usual. However, this anxiety has to be at a level that is manageable.

Of course, as we have just discussed, being prepared for the exam is half the battle right away. Attending all classes, finding out what knowledge will be expected on the exam, and knowing the exam schedules are easy steps to lowering anxiety. Keeping up with work will remove the need to cram, and efficient study habits will eliminate wasted time. Studying should be done in an ideal location for concentration, so that it is simple to become interested in the material and give it complete attention. A method such as SQ3R (Survey, Question, Read, Recite, Review) is a wonderful key to follow to make sure that the study habits are as effective as possible, especially in the case of learning from a textbook. Flashcards are great techniques for memorization. Learning to take good notes will mean that notes will be full of useful information, so that less sifting will need to be done to seek out what is pertinent for studying. Reviewing notes after class and then again on occasion will keep the information fresh in the mind. From notes that have been taken summary sheets and outlines can be made for simpler reviewing.

A study group can also be a very motivational and helpful place to study, as there will be a sharing of ideas, all of the minds can work together, to make sure that everyone understands, and the studying will be made more interesting because it will be a social occasion.

Basically, though, as long as the test-taker remains organized and self confident, with efficient study habits, less time will need to be spent studying, and higher grades will be achieved.

To become self confident, there are many useful steps. The first of these is "self talk." It has been shown through extensive research, that self-talk for students who suffer from test anxiety, should be well monitored, in order to make sure that it contributes to self confidence as opposed to sinking the student. Frequently the self talk of test-anxious students is negative or self-defeating, thinking that everyone else is smarter and faster, that they always mess up, and that if they don't do well, they'll fail the entire course. It is important to decreasing anxiety that awareness is made of self talk. Try writing any negative self thoughts and then disputing them with a positive statement instead. Begin self-encouragement as though it was a friend speaking. Repeat positive statements to help reprogram the mind to believing in successes instead of failures.

Helpful Techniques

Other extremely helpful techniques include:

Self-visualization of doing well and reaching goals

While aiming for an "A" level of understanding, don't try to "overprotect" by setting your expectations lower. This will only convince the mind to stop studying in order to meet the lower expectations.

Don't make comparisons with the results or habits of other students. These are individual factors, and different things work for different people, causing different results.

Strive to become an expert in learning what works well, and what can be done in order to improve. Consider collecting this data in a journal.

Create rewards for after studying instead of doing things before studying that will only turn into avoidance behaviors.

Make a practice of relaxing - by using methods such as progressive relaxation, self-hypnosis, guided imagery, etc - in order to make relaxation an automatic sensation.

Work on creating a state of relaxed concentration so that concentrating will take on the focus of the mind, so that none will be wasted on worrying.

Take good care of the physical self by eating well and getting enough sleep.

Plan in time for exercise and stick to this plan.

Beyond these techniques, there are other methods to be used before, during and after the test that will help the test-taker perform well in addition to overcoming anxiety.

Before the exam comes the academic preparation. This involves establishing a study schedule and beginning at least one week before the actual date of the test. By doing this, the anxiety of not having enough time to study for the test will be automatically eliminated. Moreover, this will make the studying a much more effective experience, ensuring that the learning will be an easier process. This relieves much undue pressure on the test-taker.

Summary sheets, note cards, and flash cards with the main concepts and examples of these main concepts should be prepared in advance of the actual studying time. A topic should never be eliminated from this process. By omitting a topic because it isn't expected to be on the test is only setting up the test-taker for anxiety should it actually appear on the exam. Utilize the course syllabus for laying out the topics that should be studied. Carefully go over the notes that were made in class, paying special attention to any of the issues that the professor took special care to emphasize while lecturing in class. In the textbooks, use the chapter review, or if possible, the chapter tests, to begin your review.

It may even be possible to ask the instructor what information will be covered on the exam, or what the format of the exam will be (for example, multiple choice, essay, free form, true-false). Additionally, see if it is possible to find out how many questions will be on the test. If a review sheet or sample test has been offered by the professor, make good use of it, above anything else, for the preparation for the test. Another great resource for getting to know the examination is reviewing tests from previous semesters. Use these tests to review, and aim to achieve a 100% score on each of the possible topics. With a few exceptions, the goal that you set for yourself is the highest one that you will reach.

Take all of the questions that were assigned as homework, and rework them to any other possible course material. The more problems reworked, the more skill and confidence will form as a result. When forming the solution to a problem, write out each of the steps. Don't simply do head work. By doing as many steps on paper as possible, much clarification and therefore confidence will be formed. Do this with as many homework problems as possible, before checking the answers. By checking the answer after each problem, a reinforcement will exist, that will not be on the exam. Study situations should be as exam-like as possible, to prime the test-taker's system for the experience. By waiting to check the answers at the end, a psychological advantage will be formed, to decrease the stress factor.

Another fantastic reason for not cramming is the avoidance of confusion in concepts, especially when it comes to mathematics. 8-10 hours of study will become one hundred percent more effective if it is spread out over a week or at least several days, instead of doing it all in one sitting. Recognize that the human brain requires time in order to assimilate new material, so frequent breaks and a span of study time over several days will be much more beneficial.

Additionally, don't study right up until the point of the exam. Studying should stop a minimum of one hour before the exam begins. This allows the brain to rest and put things in their proper order. This will also provide the time to become as relaxed as possible when going into the examination room. The test-taker will also have time to eat well and eat sensibly. Know that the brain needs food as much as the rest of the body. With enough food and enough sleep, as well as a relaxed attitude, the body and the mind are primed for success.

Avoid any anxious classmates who are talking about the exam. These students only spread anxiety, and are not worth sharing the anxious sentimentalities.

Before the test also involves creating a positive attitude, so mental preparation should also be a point of concentration. There are many keys to creating a positive attitude. Should fears become rushing in, make a visualization of taking the exam, doing well, and seeing an A written on the paper. Write out a list of affirmations that will bring a feeling of confidence, such as "I am doing well in my English class," "I studied well and know my material," "I enjoy this class." Even if the affirmations aren't believed at first, it sends a positive message to the subconscious which will result in an alteration of the overall belief system, which is the system that creates reality.

If a sensation of panic begins, work with the fear and imagine the very worst! Work through the entire scenario of not passing the test, failing the entire course, and dropping out of school, followed by not getting a job, and pushing a shopping cart through the dark alley where you'll live. This will place things into perspective! Then, practice deep breathing and create a visualization of the opposite situation - achieving an "A" on the exam, passing the entire course, receiving the degree at a graduation ceremony.

On the day of the test, there are many things to be done to ensure the best results, as well as the most calm outlook. The following stages are suggested in order to maximize test-taking potential:

Begin the examination day with a moderate breakfast, and avoid any coffee or beverages with caffeine if the test taker is prone to jitters. Even people who are used to managing caffeine can feel jittery or light-headed when it is taken on a test day.

Attempt to do something that is relaxing before the examination begins. As last minute cramming clouds the mastering of overall concepts, it is better to use this time to create a calming outlook.

Be certain to arrive at the test location well in advance, in order to provide time to select a location that is away from doors, windows and other distractions, as well as giving enough time to relax before the test begins.

Keep away from anxiety generating classmates who will upset the sensation of stability and relaxation that is being attempted before the exam.

Should the waiting period before the exam begins cause anxiety, create a self-distraction by reading a light magazine or something else that is relaxing and simple.

During the exam itself, read the entire exam from beginning to end, and find out how much time should be allotted to each individual problem. Once writing the exam, should more time be taken for a problem, it should be abandoned, in order to begin another problem. If there is time at the end, the unfinished problem can always be returned to and completed.

Read the instructions very carefully - twice - so that unpleasant surprises won't follow during or after the exam has ended.

When writing the exam, pretend that the situation is actually simply the completion of homework within a library, or at home. This will assist in forming a relaxed atmosphere, and will allow the brain extra focus for the complex thinking function.

Begin the exam with all of the questions with which the most confidence is felt. This will build the confidence level regarding the entire exam and will begin a quality momentum. This will also create encouragement for trying the problems where uncertainty resides.

Going with the "gut instinct" is always the way to go when solving a problem. Second guessing should be avoided at all costs. Have confidence in the ability to do well.

For essay questions, create an outline in advance that will keep the mind organized and make certain that all of the points are remembered. For multiple choice, read every answer, even if the correct one has been spotted - a better one may exist.

Continue at a pace that is reasonable and not rushed, in order to be able to work carefully. Provide enough time to go over the answers at the end, to check for small errors that can be corrected.

Should a feeling of panic begin, breathe deeply, and think of the feeling of the body releasing sand through its pores. Visualize a calm, peaceful place, and include all of the sights, sounds and sensations of this image. Continue the deep breathing, and take a few minutes to continue this with closed eyes. When all is well again, return to the test.

If a "blanking" occurs for a certain question, skip it and move on to the next question. There will be time to return to the other question later. Get everything done that can be done, first, to guarantee all the grades that can be compiled, and to build all of the confidence possible. Then return to the weaker questions to build the marks from there.

Remember, one's own reality can be created, so as long as the belief is there, success will follow. And remember: anxiety can happen later, right now, there's an exam to be written!

After the examination is complete, whether there is a feeling for a good grade or a bad grade, don't dwell on the exam, and be certain to follow through on the reward that was promised...and enjoy it! Don't dwell on any mistakes that have been made, as there is nothing that can be done at this point anyway.

Additionally, don't begin to study for the next test right away. Do something relaxing for a while, and let the mind relax and prepare itself to begin absorbing information again.

From the results of the exam - both the grade and the entire experience, be certain to learn from what has gone on. Perfect studying habits and work some more on confidence in order to make the next examination experience even better than the last one.

Learn to avoid places where openings occurred for laziness, procrastination and day dreaming.

Use the time between this exam and the next one to better learn to relax, even learning to relax on cue, so that any anxiety can be controlled during the next exam. Learn how to relax the body. Slouch in your chair if that helps. Tighten and then relax all of the different muscle groups, one group at a time, beginning with the feet and then working all the way up to the neck and face. This will ultimately relax the muscles more than they were to begin with. Learn how to breathe deeply and comfortably, and focus on this breathing going in and out as a relaxing thought. With every exhale, repeat the word "relax."

As common as test anxiety is, it is very possible to overcome it. Make yourself one of the test-takers who overcome this frustrating hindrance.

Special Report: Additional Bonus Material

Due to our efforts to try to keep this book to a manageable length, we've created a link that will give you access to all of your additional bonus material.

Please visit http://www.mometrix.com/bonus948/corrections to access the information.